THE NAVALNY CASE

Jacques Baud

THE NAVALNY CASE
Conspiracy to serve foreign policy

Max Milo

Max Milo, Paris, 2023
www.maxmilo.com
ISBN : 978-2-315-01134-6

1. Introduction

After years of fighting on the front lines against communist tyranny in the East and in the Soviet Union, I feel that we are back to square one. I see that we have acquired all the shortcomings against which we fought during the Cold War: we practice torture and censorship; we sanction without the approval of the United Nations; we interfere in the affairs of other countries and support opposition groups materially and financially; our tolerance of violations of international law is variable. In fact, we do not seek to promote our values, but use them as a tool for pressure according to our interests.

A few hours after the fall of the Berlin Wall, I was in Washington in the office of an adviser to the American President, who did not understand the significance of the event and continued to brandish the threat of a Soviet Union in full quest of power and strengthening its offensive military capabilities... In the year that followed, NATO intelligence services remained on the alert, wondering when the USSR would intervene in East Germany, as it had done in Czechoslovakia. The Americans did not understand this, because they were operating on outdated patterns.

In the early 1990s, the goal of globalization was to promote change through cooperation[1] : in a now interconnected world, the prosperity of one was to bring prosperity to the other. But this system quickly drifted. Globalization has not really translated into cooperation, but into a new division of labor in the world: Western wealth is no longer built on production, but on finance. The result is a know-how that has slowly shifted to Asia, on which we depend more and more. Since 2001, the United States has felt legitimized to intervene anywhere in the world with its Western allies and to upset the existing balance.

This has led to profound imbalances, which the Covid crisis - but not only that - highlights. Asia, led by China, is developing at high speed, Europe has relocated its companies without building an alternative economic system that enhances its own industrial capacities, and the United States is experiencing a deep crisis of innovation. After having delocalized manufacturing, we are delocalizing product engineering. As for wars, we never tire of starting them, but we are incapable of ending them. As for Russia, it is emerging very slowly from the disastrous consequences of seventy years of communism, followed by ten years of chaos and monopolization by unscrupulous oligarchs, most of whom have emigrated to Great Britain or Israel, and who have become its most bitter enemies today.

While it was relatively easy to point out the shortcomings of the Soviet Union, those of modern Russia are more difficult to identify today. Corruption, human rights abuses, economic weaknesses, etc. are mentioned, but a closer look shows that our own countries'

---

1. Erich Weede, "The Diffusion of Prosperity and Peace by Globalization," *The Independent Review*, vol. 9, n° 2, 2004, pp. 165-186 (www.jstor.org/stable/24562700), accessed 17 February 2021.

governance leaves something to be desired in these areas as well. Corruption corrodes political life in Belgium, France or Great Britain; clientelism has neglected, and then transformed immigration into an almost insoluble security problem in France; Western countries do not respect their international commitments, wage wars that are illegal and contrary to international humanitarian law; Belgium has three times and France twice as many deaths (per million inhabitants) due to Covid as Russia...

The Navalny affair is most likely not a plot, either by Russia or the United States, but a chance event that some have sought to exploit opportunistically as part of a broader strategy. It is part of a general approach, which maintains Cold War prejudices and encourages the re-emergence of nationalism in Eastern Europe.

It is indicative of worrying developments.

First, the uniformity with which it was reported in all the French-language media shows that they no longer play their role as the "fourth estate. Under the influence of the state, they have become relays of the official discourse and no longer inspire confidence.

Secondly, it illustrates a new way of looking at international relations, where diplomatic tools are abandoned in favour of pressure and sanctions. Even European countries can no longer have a completely independent policy and remain under the sword of Damocles of American sanctions. Thus, the United States does not hesitate to threaten its own allies when it seeks to implement the treaty with Iran, or complete the Nord Stream 2 project.

Third, politicians and journalists who claim to promote human rights and the rule of law are not sincere, and the people concerned know it. In Russia, their determination to promote regime change seems to work against them and to boost Russian public opinion in favor of Vladimir Putin. In other places, this same determination has only led to terrorism and the destruction of entire societies...

The problem is not the objective of promoting human rights or the rule of law, quite the contrary, but the method. For Russia (and others), our accusations are systematically based on suspicions that we have converted into "facts" by dint of repeating them and persuading ourselves of them. Even during the Cold War, although far from cordial, relations between adversaries were marked by certain values. Today, our politicians have none: corrupt, perjured and overwhelmed by the complex issues they should be solving, they take refuge in denouncing others...

2. Western conspiracy theory

First of all, it is necessary to understand what "conspiracy" (or "conspiracism") is. In the past, conspiracists were those who planned plots. Today, the term designates those who see plots everywhere, planned and implemented secretly by leaders and their secret services, with an obscure goal; their reading being seen as exclusive. Conspiracy is most often the result of an incomplete vision of events, either because the information does not exist, or because it is deliberately hidden (or classified), or because it is not sought. These "holes" in the information allow our prejudices to take hold and open the door to conspiracy.

Countries described as "authoritarian" stimulate our imagination. We readily attribute to them plots hatched by their secret services - under the occult guidance of their leaders - to eliminate individuals they do not like.

For example, it is still suggested that the murder of journalist Anna Politkovskaya in 2006 was the work of the Kremlin, although the perpetrators were members of the Chechen mafia[2]. The alleged

---

2. Alla Eshchenko, "Russian journalist's killing: 2 sentenced to life in prison," *CNN*, June 9, 2014.

"sponsors" have not been found[3], but the Russian government continues to be accused simply because the journalist was critical of it. Two years later, *France 24* claimed that Karinna Moskalenko, a lawyer for the journalist and the oligarch Mikhail Khodorkovsky, had been poisoned with mercury, suggesting an attempt at intimidation[4]. But a few days later, French investigators found that the mercury came from a thermometer accidentally broken in her car, before she bought it[5]. So nothing...

More recently, Western accusations have focused on North Korea, where opponents are constantly being eliminated... and then resurrected!

In August 2013, the French and English-speaking media echoed the propaganda of the South Korean far right and announced that North Korean leader Kim Jong-Un had allegedly had his girlfriend Hyon Song-wol shot[6]... But she reappeared in May 2014 on television! In June 2019, the British newspaper *The Mirror*[7] will note that reports of her disappearance had been *"greatly exaggerated"*... Indeed!

---

3. Tanya Lokshina, "Why Anna Politkovskaya Still Inspires," *CNN/Human Rights Watch*, October 7, 2016.
4. "L'avocate d'opposants russes empoisonnée", *France 24*, 15 October 2008.
5. "Russian lawyer 'was not poisoned'", *BBC News*, 24 October 2008; "French investigation reveals no attempt was made to poison Russia's preeminent human rights lawyer", *Bellona*, 24 October 2008.
6. "Kim Jong-un allegedly had his ex-girlfriend shot," *lepoint.fr*, August 29, 2013 (updated August 30, 2013); "North Korea: Kim Jong-un allegedly had his ex-girlfriend executed," *BFM TV*, August 30, 2013; "North Korea: Une ex de Kim Jong-un fusillée à cause d'une *sextape*," *Atlantico*, August 29, 2013; Anne-Elisabeth Celton, "Kim Jong-un allegedly had his ex-girlfriend shot over a *sex tape*," *La Tribune de Genève*, August 29, 2013; Julian Ryall, "Kim Jong-un's ex-lover 'executed by firing squad," *The Telegraph*, August 29, 2013; Kate Seamons, "Report: Kim Jong-un's ex-girlfriend executed," *USA Today*, August 29, 2013; "Death by firing squad for Kim Jong-un's ex," *CNBC*, August 29, 2013 (updated September 3, 2013).
7. Andrew Gilpin, "Kim Jong-un's pop star ex seen despite reports she was executed for making a sex tape," *mirror.co.uk*, 10 June 2019.

In May 2015, our media announced that Kim Jong-un had his aunt Kim Kyong-hui poisoned because she opposed the construction of an "acquaparc"[8]! However, in January 2020, she reappeared in public alongside Kim Jong-un, and the *BBC* even mentions that she would have a new role within the regime[9]. General Hyon Yong-chol, head of the Armed Forces, is said to have been eliminated with an anti-aircraft gun as part of *"serial executions"*[10]... but the "disappeared" reappear the next day and we learn that the general would have simply been sacked![11]

In February 2016, the Western media announced the elimination of General Ri Yong-gil, Chief of Staff of the People's Army[12] : he reappeared a few months later, at the congress of the Communist Party... with a promotion![13] On May 31, 2019, the Western media - such as the *New York Times*, *Reuters* and others - announced that Kim Jong-un *"would have had collaborators executed"* to *"take revenge"*[14]. Among them was Kim Hyok-chol, who had been one

8. J.S., "North Korea: Kim Jong-un allegedly had his aunt poisoned," *BFM TV*, May 12, 2015; Ryad Ouslimani, "Kim Jong-un allegedly had his aunt poisoned," *RTL.fr*, May 12, 2015 (updated May 13, 2015).
9. Melanie Rostagnat, "Kim Jong-un's aunt reappears in public, six years after assassination rumors," *BFM TV*, January 27, 2020; Reuters, "North Korean leader Kim Jong-un's aunt reappears after six years," *BBC News*, January 26, 2020.
10. "North Korea: the serial executions of Kim Jong-un," *Le Point.fr*, May 13, 2015.
11. "South Koreans row back over North Korea anti-aircraft gun execution claim," *The Guardian*, May 14, 2015.
12. "North Korea 'executes' army chief of staff Ri Yong-gil," *BBC News*, February 10, 2016; AFP, "North Korea: chief of staff executed," *CNews*, February 10, 2016; AFP, "North Korean army chief of staff reportedly executed," *lapresse.ca*, February 10, 2016.
13. "Un général 'exécuté' finalement bien en vie," *La Tribune de Genève*, 10 May 2016; Laura Bicker, "North Korea execution reports - why we should be cautious," *BBC News*, 31 May 2019.
14. "North Korea 'executed' officials after failed Trump summit: report," *France 24*, May 31, 2019; Choe Sang-Hun, Edward Wong, "North Korean Negotiator's Downfall Was Sealed When Trump-Kim Summit Collapsed," *The New York Times*, May 31, 2019; Hyonhee Shin, Joyce Lee, "North Korea executes envoy to failed U.S. summit -media; White House monitoring," *Reuters*, May 31, 2019.

2. Western conspiracy theory

of the negotiators at the summit with President Trump; yet, on the same day, he was seen in public while attending a performance by his wife. [15]

Same scenario with China, which has become the target of the United States with the rebound of its economy after the Covid crisis: the *"mysterious"* disappearance[16] of Jack Ma, founder and director of the online retailer Alibaba, triggers the fantasies of conspiracy theorists, who evoke a *"purge"*[17] while the day before, *Fox Business* claimed that he had not disappeared[18]. He reappeared in the media in January 2021.

In short, we don't know anything about it and we invent... For each of these "disappearances", our media and other "experts" have elaborated explanations and thus given a logic to events that have simply never taken place. This is exactly the definition of conspiracy: by believing to see conspiracies everywhere (especially where there are none), we connect facts (sometimes real) to give them an appearance of coherence. This is the mechanism used to create alternative explanations for the 9/11 attacks, the Roswell incident in 1949, or the presence of aliens in *"Area 51"* in Nevada.

Journalists and researchers do not help to bring rationality and measure back into the debate: Pascal Boniface, director of the *Institute for International and Strategic Relations* (IRIS), knows

---

15. Kim Tong-hyung, "Top North Korean official reappears days after purge report," *AP News*, June 3, 2019.

16. Julie Zaugg, "La mystérieuse disparition du patron d'Alibaba Jack Ma," *Le Temps*, January 5, 2021; "La mystérieuse disparition du milliardaire chinois Jack Ma, fondateur d'Alibaba," *L'Obs*, January 5, 2021; "Chine : comment expliquer la 'disparition' de Jack Ma, fondateur d'Alibaba ?", *RFI.fr*, January 6, 2021.

17. Marie Gingault, "Disparition de Jack Ma : il s'agit "probablement d'une purge", selon Lenglet", *RTL.fr*, 6 January 2021.

18. Susan Li, Evie Fordham, "Chinese billionaire Jack Ma's not 'missing', just 'laying low' after economic reform speech: sources," *Foc Business*, January 5, 2021.

The Navalny case

better than the CIA director[19] what provoked the Soviet intervention in Afghanistan[20] ; Renaud Girard, a journalist for Le *Figaro*, has *"proof"* that Russian agents were behind the Vrbĕtice explosion in 2014[21], while the president of the Czech Republic, Miloš Zeman, claims not to have[22] ; *Conspiracy Watch* freelancer Antoine Hasday knows better than President Barak Obama why he did not intervene after the Ghouta chemical incident in August 2013[23] and "knows" that Navalny was poisoned by Russian agents[24], while the German government has never claimed this, as we shall see.

It is understandable that the media would seek to maintain an audience by emphasizing sensationalism over accuracy. The real problem is when researchers and our governments start to adapt reality to their prejudices. For beyond the media phenomenon and journalistic ethics, this form of "conspiracy" seems to have become a foundation of our foreign policies, which increasingly boil down to the application of sanctions with disastrous effects.

The *fact-checkers* themselves are not impartial. Their role seems to be limited to highlighting and supporting "good conspiracies" (such as those that attribute conspiracies to the Russian, Chinese, Iranian governments, etc.) and to castigating "bad conspiracies" (that cast doubt on the previous ones). But this can be explained: some are simply in the service of foreign governments, as we shall see!

---

19. Robert M. Gates, *From the Shadows: The Ultimate Insider's Story of Five Presidents and How They Won the Cold War*, Simon and Schuster, 2011, p. 132.
20. Pascal Boniface, "I have read... '*Gouverner par les Fake News*' by Jacques Baud," You-Tube, September 10, 2020 (02'43"). (https://www.iris-france.org/149420-jai-lu-gouvern-er-par-les-fake-news-de-jacques-baud/).
21. Renaud Girard, "Le premier revers stratégique de Poutine," *Figaro Vox*, April 19, 2021.
22. Petr Musil, "Zeman: Nemůžeme nechat cizí agenty páchat u nás terorismus. BIS ale zatím nemá důkazy," *CNN/Prima News*, April 25, 2021.
23. Jeffrey Goldberg, "The Obama Doctrine," *The Atlantic*, April 2016.
24. Antoine Hasday, "On RT France, Jacques Baud ticks all the boxes of geopolitical conspiracism," *Conspiracy Watch*, September 7, 2020.

2. Western conspiracy theory

Paradoxically, in order to remain objective in this matter, we will base our analyses only on information provided by official services, Western media (including those financed by and serving Western governments), media linked to the Russian opposition and those considered as *"foreign agents" by the Russian authorities*. We will not consider official Russian or Russian state-funded media.

3. Who is Alexei Navalny?

The Western media present him as the *"leader"*[25] or *"leader"*[26] of the opposition. However, as an article in the *"Checknews"* section of the newspaper *Libération*[27] acknowledges, he is simply the most visible opposition figure. He is part of the so-called "off-system" opposition, made up of small groups often at the extremes of the political spectrum and too small to form parties.

Navalny began his career as a businessman in the 2000s. In accordance with a common practice in Boris Yeltsin's Russia of the 1990s and 2000s, he bought companies in order to privatize their profits (an illegal practice that led to Vladimir Putin's fight against certain oligarchs, who ended up taking refuge in Great Britain or Israel). In a first case (*Kirovles*), Navalny was sentenced to five years in prison, suspended[28].

---

25. Emmanuel Grynszpan, "Russian opponent Alexei Navalny between life and death," *Le Temps*, August 20, 2020.
26. Piotr Smolar, Benoît Vitkine, "La France prête à accueillir Alexeï Navalny, leader de l'opposition russe hospitalisé dans un état grave", *Le Monde*, 20 August 2020 (updated 21 August 2020).
27. Manuel Alaver, Xavier Condamine, "Why is Alexei Navalny presented as Vladimir Putin's main opponent?", *Libération*, September 18, 2020.
28. "Russian Activist Navalny Given 5-Year Suspended Sentence in Kirovles Retrial," *The Moscow Times*, February 8, 2017.

But the most high-profile case is the one involving the cosmetics company Yves Rocher. This is a relatively complex case, with a tangle of companies and accounts, some of them *offshore*, which is beyond the scope of this book. The best description of this case can be found in the Yves Rocher press release[29] and on Wikipedia[30] (in Russian!). In short, it is a case of personal enrichment by abuse of an official position, pitting the Russian state against Oleg Navalny, Alexei's brother. In 2008, Oleg was a manager at the automated sorting center of the Russian Post Office in Podolsk. In order to facilitate the delivery of Yves Rocher products to the sorting center, he pushed the French company to use the services of a private logistics company, *Glavpodpiska* (GPA). Problem: GPA belongs to the Navalny family. There is therefore a clear conflict of interest between the position of Oleg Navalny and GPA, which gives rise to an investigation for illegal enrichment and abuse of an official position. In addition to this case, which is similar to corruption, there are accusations of overbilling. It is important to note that Oleg Navalny is the main accused, while Alexei Navalny is "only" an accomplice. That is why Oleg was sentenced to three and a half years in prison and Alexei to three and a half years suspended[31]. It is this suspended sentence which, on appeal, is postponed - prohibiting him from leaving Russian territory - before being applied in 2021. We will come back to this.

In 2019, *Le Monde* suggests that the Russian authorities pressured the Yves Rocher company to file a complaint. The daily quotes economist Sergei Guriev, close to Navalny:

29. newsroom.yves-rocher.com/en/alexei_navalny_03_february_2021.html
30. ru.wikipedia.org/wiki/Навальный,_Алексей_Анатольевич
31. Maria Tsvetkova, "Kremlin critic Navalny given suspended sentence, brother jailed," *Reuters,* December 30, 2014.

I don't know exactly what leverage the investigators used, but it was important to them that a foreign company was involved. It made the case look solid.[32]

On February 4, *the "Matinale"* of the French-speaking Swiss radio station stated that *"the Russian authorities, who were already investigating the Navalny brothers, would have put pressure on Yves Rocher in 2012 to file a complaint against them." A case that* - according to the journalist - illustrates *"how difficult it is to be a truly free economic actor in Russia"*[33]. These are lies: on February 3, the house Yves Rocher, tired of these false accusations, has already issued a statement, where it declares:

Yves Rocher Vostok has never filed a complaint against the Navalny brothers, nor has it made any legal claim against them at any time.[34]

Oleg and Alexei Navalny took this judgment to the *European Court of Human Rights* (ECHR), arguing that it was politically motivated. Contrary to what some Western media outlets claim[35], the ECHR did not invalidate this judgment, as it did not judge the substance of the case, but its form (such as, for example, the issue of boycotting Israeli products[36]). On October 17, 2017, the ECHR issued its verdict, partially finding in favor of the two brothers on certain legal points and concluding that the Russian judiciary should pay them

---

32. Benoît Vitkine, "Procès Navalny : Yves Rocher, une plainte au service du pouvoir," *Le Monde*, December 29, 2014 (updated August 19, 2019).

33. Frédéric Mamaïs, "Alter Eco (video) - Yves Rocher et Navalny, une histoire de Sisyphe", *RTS*, 4 February 2021 (https://rts.ch/play/tv/redirect/detail/11948871?startTime=29).

34. newsroom.yves-rocher.com/en/alexei_navalny_03_february_2021.html

35. Belga, "Europe calls for Navalny's immediate release and does not rule out sanctions," *RTBF.be*, January 18, 2021.

36. Jean-Baptiste Jacquin, "Le ministère de la Justice entretient l'ambiguïté sur les appels au boycottage de produits israéliens," *Le Monde*, December 30, 2020.

3. Who is Alexei Navalny?

compensation. On the other hand, it rejected the allegation that their conviction was politically motivated (paragraph 89)[37].

In 2018, he is not allowed to run for president. *RFI* suggests that the reasons are political[38]. This is doubly untrue: on the one hand, his suspended sentence prevents him from running for office, as is the practice in other countries; on the other hand, his conviction was not politically motivated as we have seen.

Thus, and not surprisingly, our commentators, editorialists and other "experts" are making up stories.

Politically, Alexei Navalny's background is more that of an activist than a politician. In the early 2000s, as an advisor to Nikita Belykh, governor of Kirov, he was an illustrious unknown and his activism had no national or international visibility that could justify harassment by the Russian government. In 2005, he was a co-founder of the *Democratic Alternative* movement. In June 2007, he co-founded the nationalist group *Narod* ("People"), which was not very successful. In June 2008, it merged with two other Russian nationalist movements: the *Movement Against Illegal Immigration* (MAII) (whose logo is reminiscent of the 1930s[39]) and *Great Russia*, to form a new coalition: the *Russian National Movement*.

In 2010, on the recommendation of Garry Kasparov, Navalny was invited to the United States to participate in the *Yale World Fellows Program*. This is a fifteen-week non-degree training program offered by Yale University to foreigners, identified by some American elites as "future leaders" in their respective countries.

---

37. ECHR, *Case of Navalnyye V. Russia (Application No. 101/15), Judgment*, Strasbourg, 17 October 2017 (Final 5 March 2018) (hudoc.echr.coe.int/eng?i=001-177665)
38. "Russia: Alexei Navalny banned from running for president in 2018", *rfi.fr*, 25 December 2017.
39. Article "Movement against illegal immigration", *Wikipedia*.

Back in Russia, Navalny advocates for the rights of small shareholders in large companies and denounces abuses in corporate practices. His *Anti-Corruption Fund* (FBK) attracts sympathy, but also a lot of distrust and antipathy. This is used to portray him as a democrat, but that is far from the case. In 2016, the Public Prosecutor's Office of the Swiss Confederation dropped a complaint it had improperly filed against Artiom Chaika, son of Russia's general prosecutor[40]. In 2017, Russian billionaire Alisher Usmanov, filed a libel suit against Navalny and won his case[41]. In 2018, Navalny loses a libel suit against businessman Mikhail Prokhorov[42].

As for his ideas, the picture is not much better. In 2007, he was expelled from the center-right Yabloko party because of his regular participation in the *"Russian March"*, an ultranationalist movement, and his *"nationalist activities"* with racist tendencies[43]. At that time, in a video for the liberalization of handguns, which became famous, he mimes shooting Chechen migrants in Russia[44]. In October 2013, he supported[45] and fanned[46], the Biryulyovo riots, castigating the *"hordes of legal and illegal*

40. Yuri Chaika, Prosecutor General of Russia will be relieved of his duties by Vladimir Putin, for suspicion of corruption.

41. "Russian tycoon Usmanov sues Navalny for libel," *BBC News*, April 13, 2017; Associated Press, "Russian opposition leader Navalny loses defamation case," *Taiwan News*, May 31, 2017.

42. "Russian Court Orders Navalny To Retract Bribery Allegation Against Tycoon Prokhorov," *RFE/RL*, June 26, 2018.

43. Robert Coalson, "Is Aleksei Navalny a Liberal or a Nationalist?", *The Atlantic*, July 29, 2013.

44. Video "НАРОД (ЗА легализацию оружия" ("Narod for the legalization of firearms"), *Alexey Navalny/YouTube*, September 19, 2007 (youtube.com/watch?v=oVN-JiO10SWw).

45. Sean Guillory, "How Russian Nationalism Fuels Race Riots," *The Nation*, 1ᵉʳ November 2013.

46. Simon Shuster, "Russia Responds to Anti-Migrant Riots by Arresting Migrants," *Time Magazine*, October 14, 2013.

immigrants." In 2017, the American media *Salon*, close to the Democratic Party, says that *"if he were American, liberals would hate Navalny much more than they hate Trump or Steve Bannon"*[47]. In 2017, the American media outlet *Jacobin*, close to the left wing of the Democratic Party, even called him a *"Russian Trump"*[48]. In fact, as the *American Foreign Policy Magazine* of the American University of Princeton noted in December 2018, he emerged through far-right groups, and his ideas are more akin to what is described as *"populist"* in the West[49]. We recommend the reader to watch the interview with two left-wing "anti-Putin" activists, conducted by the American media outlet *The Grayzone*, which illustrates the partisan (and very undemocratic) nature with which our media represents him[50].

On *France 5*, the Moscow correspondent of Le Monde explains that this is *"the first Navalny"*[51], suggesting that there would be a second - different - Navalny today. The same is true of the *Swiss Radio-Television* (RTS) program *"Géopolitis"* of February 21, 2021, devoted to Navalny: the presenter states that *"from his ultranationalist beginnings and his anti-migrant declarations, with Navalny there is practically nothing left"*[52]. This is not true: in April 2017, he confided to a *Guardian* journalist that he had not changed

47. Danielle Ryan, "Dictator vs. democrat? Not quite: Russian opposition leader Alexey Navalny is no progressive hero," *Salon*, April 2, 2017.
48. Per Leander, Alexey Sakhnin, "Russia's Trump," *jacobinmag.com*, July 11, 2017.
49. Misha Tseitlin, "End Capital Punishment: The Short-sightedness of Magnitsky Act Sanctions on Kadyrov," *American Foreign Policy Magazine*, December 22, 2018.
50. Aaron Maté, "For Russian leftists, Western favorite Navalny represents same corrupt elitism," *The Grayzone/YouTube.com*, February 10, 2021.
51. Benoît Vitkine, in the program " C dans l'air " of January 28, 2021, ("Poutine/Navalny: espion, poison et corruption", *France 5/YouTube*, January 29, 2021) (58'10")
52. "Putin-Navalny, the duel", *Géopolitis/RTS.ch*, February 21, 2021 (04'15") (rts.ch/play/tv/geopolitis/video/putin-navalny-le-duel?urn=urn:rts:video:11987915)

his opinion[53]. In October 2020, he repeated the same thing to the German magazine *Der Spiegel*[54] :

> Guardian: *You were expelled by a party because of your participation in a Russian nationalist march in Moscow. Have your views changed?*
> Navalny: *I have the same opinions as when I entered politics.*

In order to attract votes from the extremes on the right and left - not enough to field candidates separately - Navalny applied the concept of *smart voting*. European parliamentarian Bernard Guetta credits him with inventing it[55]. But Navalny did not "invent" anything, he was inspired by American *strategic* or *tactical voting*. While in France the "*useful vote*" consists in giving one's vote to the candidate who is closest to one's opinions, the principle of Navalny's "*smart voting*" is to give one's vote to anyone, *except* to a member of *United Russia* (Vladimir Putin's party). It works on a different logic: it is not based on a *preference*, but on a *detestation*... Quite a symbol!

The advantage of this process is that it allows to gather the votes of extremists. This explains Navalny's "success" in the 2013 Moscow municipal elections, where "he" got 27%[56] of the vote. But this is a deceptive success: it does not express a *preference* for Navalny, but a *rejection of* the then incumbent mayor of Moscow. The disadvantage

53. Shaun Walker, "Alexei Navalny on Putin's Russia: 'All autocratic regimes come to an end,'" *The Guardian*, April 29, 2017.
54. Benjamin Bidder, Christian Esch, "I Assert that Putin Was Behind the Crime," *spiegel. de*, October 1st 2020.
55. Bernard Guetta in the program "C à vous", February 3, 2021, *France 5/YouTube*, February 3, 2021) (13'30").
56. Will Englund, "Kremlin critic Alexei Navalny has strong showing in Moscow mayoral race, despite loss," *The Washington Post*, September 9, 2013.

3. Who is Alexei Navalny?

is that Navalny's supporters are a very disparate, often unnatural assembly, where internal rivalries are very strong.

But this also shows that its supporters do not gather around a project *for* Russia, but around a determination *against* the "power", illustrating the Western approach: it is not about promoting an improvement for Russia, but on the contrary, its weakening.

In reality, Navalny's popularity is very low. A poll conducted between August 20 and 26, 2020 (just after his "poisoning") by the *Levada Center*[57] (financed by the Americans and considered in Russia as a *"foreign agent"*[58], so not really *"affiliated with the regime"*) shows the difference in popularity between Vladimir Putin and Alexei Navalny (see Table 1).

---

57. "Доверие политикам и президентское голосование" ("Trust in politicians and presidential voting intentions"), *levada.ru*, September 3, 2020.
58. "Russia's Levada Centre polling group named foreign agent," *BBC News*, September 5, 2016.

	Apr. 2014	Jan. 2016	Apr 2017	Jan. 2018	March 2019	July 2019	Dec. 2019	August 2020	Nov. 2020
Vladimir Putin	60	66	62	70	55	54	53	56	55
Vladimir Zhirinovsky	5	3	4	5	6	4	6	5	9
Gennady Zyuganov	5	5	3	1	2	1	3	2	2
Alexei Navalny	‹ 1	1	1	‹ 1	1	1	2	2	2
Mikhail Mishoustin	-	-	-	-	-	-	-	2	1
Pavel Gurdinin	-	-	-	6	5	4	4	2	1
Sergei Choigou	1	2	1	‹1	1	1	1	1	1
Nikolai Platoshkin	-	-	-	-	-	-	-	1	1
Other	3	2	3	2	4	2	3	3	4
I do not know	26	21	25	15	25	31	27	27	23

Table 1 - Voting intentions in November 2020 (among voters who planned to vote). August 2020 figures are from a poll conducted in the week of August 20-26, 2020, which was after the Navalny "poisoning attempt." [Source: "Президентские электоральные рейтинги и уровень доверия политикам" ("Voting Intentions in the Presidential Election and Level of Confidence in Politicians"), levada.ru, Dec. 10, 2020].

4. The case

4.1. Poisoning

On Thursday, August 20, 2020, during his flight from Tomsk to Moscow, the opponent Alexei Navalny is taken by violent pain. The flight is diverted to Omsk so that he can be hospitalized urgently.

At this stage, no analysis has been carried out and no one knows the exact nature of Navalny's illness, but his spokesperson says he was deliberately poisoned[59]. The rumors circulating on social networks about the consumption of alcohol combined with drugs are immediately described as *"defamatory"* by our media[60]. They are already preferred, without any supporting evidence, to a more romantic version: a poisoning with Novitchok on the orders of Putin[61].

---

59. twitter.com/Kira_Yarmysh/status/1296293654462685185
60. Emmanuel Grynszpan, "Russian opponent Alexei Navalny between life and death," *Le Temps*, August 20, 2020.
61. Normand Lester, "Alexeï Navalny poisoned on orders from Putin?", *Le Journal de Montréal*, August 20, 2020; Emmanuel Grynszpan, "L'opposant russe Alexeï Navalny entre la vie et la mort", *Le Temps*, August 20, 2020; Alain Barluet, "Russie : l'opposant Alexeï Navalny, cible d'un possible empoisonnement", *Le Figaro*, August 20, 2020; Magalie Letissier, "Russie. Poisoned, shot dead... The long list of silenced opponents", *Ouest-France*, 20 August 2020.

Assuming that there was a deliberate (and therefore criminal) poisoning, its course still remains a mystery nine months later, and explanations have varied. In a first version, his entourage affirms that he was poisoned[62] by drinking tea[63] at the airport of Tomsk[64]. The problem is that the tea was brought to him by Ilya Pakhomov, one of his colleagues[65]. Later, another video will show a waitress putting cups on the table[66], so we don't know.

His entourage then evoked a second version: poisoning with water bottles in the hotel[67], which Navalny's team (who remained in Tomsk) recovered on August 20[68]. The British media *The Sun* publishes the video of the operation, taking care to erase the appeals of the chambermaid not to touch anything before the arrival of the police, in order to hide the fact that the alleged crime scene has been altered[69]. From then on, the integrity of the chain of custody is no longer assured; something that conspiracy theorists will obviously not mention. Navalny's entourage claims to have taken the bottles to Germany for analysis. But scans of the Navalny team's luggage at the boarding gate, published by the private Russian media REN TV[70], confirm that there were no bottles (which would have been confiscated anyway), while surveillance cameras show one of Navalny's relatives buying water from a vending machine

62. "No poison in Navalny's system," *Tribune de Genève*, August 21, 2020.
63. twitter.com/Kira_Yarmysh/status/1296296624831029258
64. Joël Chatreau, "Alexei Navalny, 'bête noire' of Russian President Putin, was 'poisoned' according to his entourage," *euronews.fr*, 20 August 2020.
65. youtu.be/CV1aYLenCMk
66. youtu.be/SIoUF7vfliY
67. Sebastian Shukla, Vasco Cotovio, Mary Ilyushina, "Novichok found on water bottle suggests Russia's Navalny poisoned before he went to airport, aides say," *CNN*, September 17, 2020.
68. www.instagram.com/p/CFOnffrHZ0d/
69. youtu.be/46haO3h_TVI
70. REN TV is 30% owned by the RTL group.

after the luggage check[71]. In September 2020, one of Navalny's associates himself confessed that the water bottle was not the cause of the poisoning[72] ! In any case, according to the *BBC*, Navalny would not have ingested anything other than his tea at the airport that morning[73]. In short, we don't know anything about it!...

Voluntarily or not, but clearly, Navalny's supporters have contributed to the opacity of the case. One could be surprised that these bottles were not transmitted to the Russian doctors who treated Navalny in Omsk, nor to the German doctors, in order to facilitate - theoretically - his treatment... With supporters like that, Navalny does not need Putin!

Navalny's entourage then put forward a third version: the poisoning of Navalny's underpants[74], "revealed" during a telephone conversation with what is presented to us as an *"FSB* [Federal Security Service] *agent"*, broadcast in a loop on the Western media[75]. We will come back to this in more detail.

4.1.1. Novitchok

Novitchok (the name means *"Little New One"*) was revealed to the general public by the Skripal case in 2018. It is a little-known combat toxicant, some technical details of which were published in 2008 in

71. "МВД показало, как помощница Навального купила бутылку в аэропорту" ("Interior Ministry showed how Navalny's aide bought a bottle at the airport"), *ren.tv*, October 8, 2020.
72. "Nawalnys Team zur Vergiftung: 'Die Flasche war wohl nicht die Quelle des Giftes'" ("Nawalny's team on poisoning: 'The bottle was probably not the source of the poison'"), *Der Tagesspiegel*, September 17, 2020.
73. BBC Russian, "Alexei Navalny: Two hours that saved Russian opposition leader's life," *BBC News*, September 3, 2020.
74. Tim Lister, Clarissa Ward, Sebastian Shukla, "Russian opposition leader Alexey Navalny dupes spy into revealing how he was poisoned," *CNN*, December 21, 2020.
75. *Video* "Я позвонил своему убийце. Он признался" ("I called my killer. He confessed"), *Алексей Навальный/YouTube*, December 21, 2020 (youtube.com/watch?v=ibqiet6Bg38).

4. The case

the book by Vil *Mirzayanov*, one of its designers[76]. It is a combat toxicant that remained at the experimental stage and was *never* adopted by the USSR/Russia. It was developed in the 1970s-1980s by the Chikhany (Russia) and Nukus (now Uzbekistan) laboratories, and should have been produced by the Pavlodar Laboratory (now in Kazakhstan). Noting that its high toxicity made it difficult to handle on the battlefield, the Soviets abandoned its development, and these facilities were converted to produce chemicals for civilian use in 1987.

In December 1991, Kazakhstan declared its independence and the Pavlodar site was dismantled under the supervision of the United States. At that time, all the sites closely or remotely involved in the development, testing or production of Novitchok were dismantled.

This is why, even after its formula became known to the West, Novitchok was not included in the *Organization for the Prohibition of Chemical Weapons* (OPCW) list of chemical weapons. This explains why the OPCW did not spontaneously intervene in the Skripal case in 2018. It was only after this case, in November 2019, that this toxic was added to the list. At Russia's request, the formulas of four Novitchok-related agents were then added to the OPCW's list of banned products[77].

After the incident with Navalny, Western countries protested against the use of chemical weapons in Europe, in violation of international law[78]. Yet, the German government's October 6 press release states that *"this publicly unknown nerve agent has not yet*

---

76. Vil S. Mirzayanov, *State Secrets: An Insider's Chronicle of the Russian Chemical Weapons Program*, Outskirts Press, Inc, 2008.
77. Davide Castelvecchi, "Novichok nerve agents banned by chemical-weapons treaty," *Nature*, November 28, 2019.
78. *Council Decision (Pesc) 2020/1482 of 14 October 2020 amending Decision (Pesc) 2018/1544 on restrictive measures to combat the proliferation and use of chemical weapons*, European Union, 15 October 2020.

been officially listed by the OPCW[79]"... And it does not appear that it will be in the future, as we shall see.

According to the German newspapers *Süddeutsche Zeitung*[80] and *Die Zeit*[81], in the early 1990s, the German intelligence service, the BND, succeeded in obtaining samples of Novitchok for analysis in several Nato countries[82], including Germany[83], the United States, Great Britain, Czechoslovakia and Sweden[84], for the purpose of research and development of antidotes. Thus, since the early 1990s, the United States has filed nearly 140 patents on chemical weapons of this type. As early as 1998, the American chemical weapons laboratory in Edgewood synthesized Novitchok[85]. According to Nikolai Kovalyov, a former FSB director and Duma deputy, a small stockpile of Novitchok existed in Ukraine[86].

In addition, as early as 1994, the Russian government prosecuted Leonid Rink, a former employee of the *National Research Institute of Organic Chemistry and Technology* (GosNIIOKhT), for working on Novitchok and diverting small amounts of it for sale

79. "Erklärung der Bundesregierung im Fall Nawalny" ("Statement of the Federal Government on the Navalny Case"), Pressemitteilung 356, *Presse- und Informationsamt der Bundesregierung* (BPA), 6 October 2020.
80. Georg Mascolo, Holger Stark, "BND beschaffte Nervengift "Nowitschok" in den 90er Jahren" ("BND procured nerve agent "Novichok" in the 1990s"), *Süddeutsche Zeitung*, 16 May 2018.
81. "BND beschaffte Nowitschok aus russischem Labor" ("BND procured Novitchok from a Russian laboratory"), *Die Zeit*, May 16, 2018.
82. Samuel Osborne, "Germany obtained novichok nerve agent sample in 1990s, reports say," *The Independent*, May 17, 2018.
83. Alexander Pearson, "Skripal poisoning: Germany got Novichok chemical sample from Russia in 1990s," *dw.com*, 17 May 2018.
84. "West's knowledge of Novichok came from sample secured in 1990s: report," *Reuters*, 16 May 2018.
85. Karel Knip, "Unknown'newcomer novichok was long known," *nrc.nl*, 21 March 2018.
86. Tony Wesolowsky, "A Timeline Of Russia's Changing Story On Skripal Poisoning," *Radio Free Europe / Radio Liberty*, March 21, 2018.

4. The case

to members of the Latvian mafia[87]. In order to support the theory of a Russian government conspiracy, conspiracy theorists deny[88] even the claims of the *New York Times*[89] that the Russian mafia had already used a variant of Novitchok to murder Ivan Kivelidi of *Rosbusinessbank* in 1995[90].

This "proliferation" explains why Leonid Rink claims on the official Russian media *RIA Novosti*, that *"the British could have poisoned Skripal"*[91]. Even if this is most probably not the case, he is not wrong either, because honesty should force us to recognize that Novitchok has not been a Russian exclusive for a long time. Thus, the categorical attribution of its use to the Russian government is highly questionable.

As for GosNIIOKhT, which is suspected of producing Novitchok, it is under the supervision of the Ministry of Trade and Industry. It deals with *"research on ecological safety and human risk analysis, and carries out several activities in the civil chemical industry and environmental protection"*, and its access is monitored by two unarmed guards, as journalists from the British *Telegraph* noted shortly after the Skripal affair...[92]

---

87. "Secret trial shows risks of nerve agent theft in post-Soviet chaos: experts," *Reuters*, March 14, 2018.
88. Antoine Hasday, *op. cit.*
89. Alessandra Stanley, "Moscow Journal; To the Business Risks in Russia, Add Poisoning," *The New York Times*, August 9, 1995.
90. Roman Shleinov, "Новичок" уже убивал" ("Novichok" has already killed"), *Novaya Gazeta*, March 22, 2018.
91. Andrei Veselo, "Отравить Скрипаля могли британцы" ("The British may have poisoned Skripal"), *RIA Novosti*, 20 March 2018.
92. Alexander Bratersky, "Revealed: The Moscow weapons lab that made the deadly Novichok nerve agent," *The Telegraph*, July 5, 2018.

Moreover, the very existence of a Novitchok development program is disputed by Russia[93] and some Western experts[94]. There is no conspiracy here, but there is a confusion of terms: first of all, the designation Novitchok does not seem to have been official, but only a common nickname; secondly, "Agent A" is confused with the development of another category of toxic agents, designated "GV agents". Without getting into this very technical debate, we will use the term Novitchok here, as it is generally understood in the West.

4.1.2. Mode of action

To understand the bias with which the Western media has presented the case, it is important to know the nature of the poison that is assumed to have been used.

Novitchok is the nickname given to a range of chemical toxins developed on an experimental basis in the USSR during the 1970s and 1980s under the generic code name FOLIANT. It is an organophosphorus toxicant of the category of innervating toxicants (or neurotoxicants), which act by disrupting the functioning of muscles.

Our muscles contract thanks to a neurotransmitter: acetylcholine (ACh), released in the synapses of the motor nerves. They relax due to the effect of an enzyme that "neutralizes" acetylcholine: acetylcholinesterase (AChE). Neurotoxins work by inhibiting AChE. In other words, the muscles contract and do not relax: a generalized cramp blocks the heart and breathing, causing death within a very short time.

In the context of the Navalny case, it is important to point out that AChE inhibitors are not specific to combat neurotoxins. They are also found in insecticides (from which combat toxins were deve-

---

93. Video "Zakharova about the Moscow's response to London's actions," *Rossiya24*, March 18, 2018 (youtube.com/watch?v=vTA6KA3fCzc).
94. Paul McKeigue, Jake Mason, Piers Robinson, "Update to briefing note 'Doubts about Novichoks," *Timhayward*, 1st April 2018.

loped) and in certain treatments for neurological diseases, such as Parkinson's and Alzheimer's, as well as in psychiatry and in many drugs. They do not have the same virulence as nerve agents, but may show similar biomarkers in the blood.

There are several kinds of neurotoxins, which are distinguished by their toxicity, persistence and form:

- *G-agents* (such as sarin), developed in the 1930s-1950s and "less" toxic;

- *V-agents* (such as VX), developed in the 1960s-1970s, which are slightly more toxic;

- *Novitchok-type* agents (*A-agents*), which have a very low lethal dose and can kill an individual in less than two minutes. This is a family of products, the main ones being: substance 33, A-230, A-232, A-234, A-242 and A-262[95].

Neurotoxins act through inhalation and skin contact. Their effects may vary according to the individual.

Toxic	Type	Lethal Dose1 LD50 [g/person]
Sarin	agent G	1,700
Soman		0,350
VX	agent V	0,010
A-232	agent A (Novitchok)	0,001-0,002
A-234		0,005

Table 2 - Toxicity of nerve agents (innervants) by skin contact for a 70 kg person. Lethal doses from inhalation are about ten times lower. For this reason, the handling of intoxicated objects or persons must be done with special protection. [Source: Eugenie Nepovimovaa and Kamil Kucab, "Chemical warfare agent NOVICHOK - mini-review of available data," Food and Chemical Toxicology, Vol. 121, November 2018, pp. 343-350]

---

95. Peter R. Chai, Bryan D. Hayes, Timothy B. Erickson, Edward W. Boyer, "Novichok agents: a historical, current, and toxicological perspective," *Toxicology Communications*, 2:1, 2018, pp. 45-48, (DOI: 10.1080/24734306.2018.1475151).

Neurotoxins were developed for combat and act so quickly that hospitalization is usually not possible. This is why, in all western armies, soldiers are equipped - in case of war - with devices allowing them to inject atropine within *seconds* of poisoning, in order to neutralize its effects.

The particularity of Novitchoks is that they degrade AChE in an *irreversible* way[96] and are thus the most virulent neurotoxins. As their effects are rapidly irreversible, it is essential to wear a special waterproof suit with a gas mask when in contact with intoxicated people or objects. However, the images of Navalny's arrival in Germany do not show any special protective measures for the flight and accompanying personnel. This will arouse the astonishment of some members of parliament, who will question the government on the measures taken to allow the entry of potentially intoxicated persons and objects into Germany. The government simply replied *"that it has no information on this subject"*[97]. Surprising!

Assuming that Navalny was poisoned with Novitchok, the Latvian-based opposition media *Meduza* notes that this was far from the best choice[98]. Novitchok was designed as a combat toxicant: it is not intended to be discreet, but to be effective! As *Meduza* points out, there are many, many more effective and discreet poisons[99].

96. Eugenie Nepovimovaa and Kamil Kucab, "Chemical warfare agent NOVICHOK - mini-review of available data," *Food and Chemical Toxicology*, Vol. 121, November 2018, pp. 343-350.
97. *Antwort der Bundesregierung auf die Kleine Anfrage der Abgeordneten Dr. Anton Friesen, Armin-Paulus Hampel, Dr. Roland Hartwig, weiterer Abgeordneter und der Fraktion der AfD- Drucksache 19/23352 - Offene Fragen bezüglich des mutmaßlichen Anschlags auf Alexej Nawalny*, Deutscher Bundestag, Drucksache 19/24493, November 19, 2020 (questions 4, 6 and 69).
98. "Highly toxic, but unreliable *Meduza* answers key questions about Novichok-type nerve agent poisoning," *meduza.io*, September 3, 2020.
99. "There are better poisons if you really want to kill someone" The chemical weapons expert who led the OPCW's mission to Salisbury after the Novichok attack on the Skripals explains Alexey Navalny's situation", *meduza.io*, 3 September 2020.

4. The case

However, all those who are suspected of having been the object of a Novitchok attack are still alive! This will lead Agnès Callamard and Irene Khan, two "experts" of the United Nations[100], to affirm - without proving it - that it was a warning[101]. An idea that the OPCW expert quoted by *Meduza* had already beaten, because the lethal quantities are so minute that it is almost impossible to measure the poison.

The question could then be: *was Novitchok really discovered?*

4.1.3. The Western narrative

At no time have our media or "experts" questioned the initial hypothesis of an assassination attempt ordered by Vladimir Putin. On *France 5*, five months after the "poisoning attempt", François Clémenceau states:

> He was poisoned with a chemical weapon [...] that was manu-
> factured in laboratories sophisticated enough to suggest that
> Russian services are necessarily behind it.[102]

It contradicts the journal *Nature*, according to which these toxics can be easily produced: it is their weaponization that is complicated[103]. In fact, the "certainties" established during the Skripal case in 2018 are repeated. Yet, the British accusations were already very

---

100. Agnès Callamard is Special Rapporteur on extrajudicial, summary or arbitrary executions, and Irene Khan is Special Rapporteur on the promotion and protection of freedom of opinion and expression.
101. Agnès Callamard and Irene Khan, "Mandates of the Special Rapporteur on extrajudicial, summary or arbitrary executions; and the Special Rapporteur on the promotion and protection of the right to freedom of opinion and expression," *un.org*, December 30, 2020 (AL RUS 11/2020).
102. François Clémenceau in the program "C dans l'air" of February 3, 2020, ("Can Navalny bring down Putin? #cdanslair 03.02. 2020 ", *France 5/YouTube*, February 4, 2021) (29'25").
103. Leiv K. Sydnes, "Nerve agents: from discovery to deterrence," *Nature*, 30 June 2020 (doi: https://doi.org/10.1038/d41586-020-01910-8)

fragile then. The *Salisbury Journal* of March 5, 2018, mentioned a possible intoxication with *fentanyl*[104] ; information taken up in September 2018 by *Radio Free Europe/Radio Liberty,* which specified that the report of the Skripals' admission to hospital mentioned *fentanyl* intoxication, without naming Novitchok[105]. On March 16, 2018, a *National Health Service* emergency medicine consultant confirmed that *"no patients showed symptoms of nerve agent poisoning in Salisbury and there were only three cases of serious poisoning"*[106].

Even Theresa May had to admit that the accusation against Russia was only *circumstantial:*

> *Based on [its] capability, coupled with its history of state-sponsored assassinations - including against former intelligence officers whom they consider legitimate targets - the British government concluded that it was highly likely that Russia was responsible for this irresponsible and despicable act.*[107]

In other words, the accusation was not based on findings, but on the assumption that Russia has the capacity to produce the poison; but it is still not known whether the *"toxic substance"* *actually* originated in Russia[108]. For this reason, Gary Aitkenhead, director of the *Defence Science and Technology Laboratory* (DSTL) at Porton Down, which had analyzed the Skripal toxin, objected to the British govern-

---

104. "Man found critically ill at Maltings in Salisbury man is former Russian spy Sergei Skripal," *salisburyjournal.co.uk,* 5 March 2018.
105. Ron Synovitz, "Name Your Poison: Exotic Toxins Fell Kremlin Foes," *Radio Free Europe/Radio Liberty*, September 18, 2018.
106. Fiona Hamilton, John Simpson & Deborah Haynes, "Russia: Salisbury poison fears allayed by doctor," *The Times*, March 16, 2018
107. Theresa May, March 14, 2018 (quoted in presentation at the British Embassy in Moscow to the diplomatic corps on March 22, 2018).
108. AFP-Reuters, "Britisches Institut fand keine Quelle für Skripal-Gift" ("British Institute found no source for Skripal poison"), *Zeit.de*, April 3, 2018.

ment's reference to a toxin *"produced"* or *"manufactured"* by Russia, and agreed only with the wording "of *a type developed by Russia.*

On March 12, 2018, before Parliament, Theresa May will therefore use this formulation that expresses the doubts of the Porton Down laboratory:

> *It is now clear that Mr. Skripal and his daughter were poisoned with a military-grade nerve agent of a type developed by Russia.*[109]

This same expression was used in the joint communiqué issued by the United States, Great Britain, Germany and France on 15 March to condemn Russia's action[110]. The British ambassador to the OPCW summarized the situation very well:

> *[Neither the DSTL analysis nor the OPCW report identifies the country or laboratory of origin of the agent used in this attack. So let me also present the bigger picture, which leads the UK to believe that there is no plausible explanation for what happened in Salisbury other than Russian state responsibility.*[111]

This will not prevent Boris Johnson from lying by saying that Aitkenhead had confirmed the Russian origin of Novitchok. The *Foreign Office* will relay the information in a tweet... which will be quickly deleted[112].

---

109. "PM Commons statement on Salisbury incident: 12 March 2018," gov.uk, 12 March 2018.
110. Alex Ward, "The US and 3 allies are blaming Russia for nerve agent attack on ex-spy," *vox.com*, March 15, 2018.
111. *Statement By H.E. Ambassador Peter Wilson Permanent Representative Of The United Kingdom Of Great Britain And Northern Ireland To The OPCW At The Fifty-Ninth Meeting Of The Executive Council*, OPCW Executive Council, 18 April 2018 (EC-M-59/NAT.6).
112. "Foreign Office deletes tweet claiming Salisbury nerve agent made in Russia," *SkyNews*, April 4, 2018.

This is simplistic logic, to say the least, and shows that sanctions against Russia were adopted without any material evidence that the toxic agent was of Russian origin and that it was hired by Russian agents.

Moreover, on March 22, 2018, in a document to authorize the OPCW to obtain blood samples from the Skripals, the British judge is even less categorical:

> *Blood samples from Sergei Skripal and Yulia Skripal were analyzed and the results indicated exposure to a nerve agent* or related compound. *The samples tested positive for the presence of a Novitchok class nerve agent* or a closely related agent.[113]

In 2020, an OPCW document classified as *OPCW HIGHLY PROTECTED* (equivalent to "secret") leaked to the Austrian press. Authenticated by its barcode, the document was probably leaked by the *Bundesamt für Verfassungsschutz und Terrorismusbekämpfung* (BVT), the internal security service. It reveals the formula of the toxic agent identified by the OPCW, showing that it was not Novitchok and that the British government simply invented the accusations against Russia[114]. But obviously, no media in France relayed the information...

Thus, not only the Russian origin of the poison could not be determined, but its very nature is not identified with precision! The symptoms described in the press are similar to those of intoxication by *paralytic shellfish poisoning* (PSP), also known as *saxitoxin* (STX),

---

113. *Approved Judgment*, Royal Courts of Justice, Strand, London, WC2A 2LL, 22 March 2018.
114. johnhelmer.net/austria-confirms-opcw-report-on-skripal-faking-by-the-british-vienna-exposes-financial-times-lies-and-cover-up/

4. The case

produced by marine micro-organisms[115]. This is why the hypothesis of a food poisoning of the Skripals by seafood - as suggested by the emergency doctor of the Salisbury hospital - remains the most likely hypothesis... But that *Conspiracy Watch* considers as conspiracy[116]!

Three years later, no element has come to reinforce the hypothesis of Russian guilt, on the contrary. But the media - and the European parliamentarians - have been able to use the carefully nurtured vagueness and uncertainty to make an accusation against Russia in the Navalny case, without any material evidence. Moreover, we can see that the German government is in the same uncertainty as the British two years ago. Despite the firm tone of their September 2, 2020 communiqué, the Germans are not accusing the Russian government:

> *It is shocking that Alexei Navalny was the victim of a nerve agent attack in Russia.*
> *The federal government condemns this attack in the strongest possible terms.*
> *The Russian government is invited to explain the incident.*[117]

Therefore, to claim that it was a *"state assassination*[118] "* is a lie based on an extrapolation that the German government never made. In short: conspiracy in the true sense of the word.

---

115. STX is a nerve agent that the United States attempted to weaponize in the 1960s for special operations. During its investigation into the CIA's clandestine activities in 1975, the Church Commission discovered that the Agency kept a stockpile of it. (We are not suggesting here that the CIA was involved in the Skripal case!)
116. Antoine Hasday, *op. cit.*
117. "Erklärung der Bundesregierung im Fall Nawalny" ("Statement of the Federal Government on the Navalny Case"), Pressemitteilung 306, *Presse- und Informationsamt der Bundesregierung* (BPA), September 2, 2020.
118. François Clémenceau in the program "C dans l'air", February 3, 2020 ("Can Navalny bring down Putin? #cdanslair 03.02.2020", *France 5/YouTube*, February 4, 2021) (29'55").

4.2. Hospitalization and transport in Germany

On August 20, shortly after Navalny arrived at the hospital in Omsk, Russian doctors thought - at first - that he had been poisoned. About ten minutes after his arrival at the hospital, they administered atropine. As atropine is a product used as an antidote in case of poisoning by nerve agents, some conspiracy theorists[119] see it as proof that the doctors "knew" that he had been poisoned by Novitchok. This is obviously false, because if this had been the case, the medical staff in Omsk would have welcomed him with adequate protective equipment!

In fact, atropine is used in many medical situations, including intubation, as explained by the Russian opposition media *Meduza*[120]. On *Radio Free Europe/Radio Liberty*, Dr. Aleksandr Sabayev explains that doctors quickly realized that it was a metabolic problem and gave him atropine at a much lower dose than that used in cases of poisoning[121].

But the conspiracy theory persists: it is suggested that he is in a coma because of his poisoning before arriving at the hospital in Omsk[122]. The Belgian media *Sudinfo.be* claims that Navalny "*[was] medically transferred [to Germany] after falling into a coma after returning from a trip to Siberia, a victim of alleged poisoning*"[123]. This is disinformation.

119. Galia Ackerman, in the program "C dans l'air" of September 5, 2020, ("Poutine, l'opposant et le poison #cdanslair 05.09.20", *France 5/YouTube*, September 7, 2020) (07'34").
120. "We're in the business of saving lives, get it?", *meduza.io*, 28 August 2020.
121. "Омский токсиколог: врачи скорой не вводили Навальному атропин" ("Omsk toxicologist: paramedics did not administer atropine to Navalny"), *Radio Svoboda*, October 7, 2020 (svoboda.org/a/30880019.html).
122. "Poisoned, Russian opponent Alexei Navalny is in a coma," *RTS.ch*, August 20, 2020.
123. Belga, "Germany has passed the Navalny court case to Moscow," *Sudinfo.be*, January 16, 2021.

In fact, it was the Russian doctors who decided to put him in an artificial coma in order to facilitate his oxygenation (as it is done for the patients of Covid-19). This explains the products found in his blood shortly afterwards, which are shown in the protocols of the Omsk hospital quoted by *Meduza*[124] :

> *Found in blood: propofol, pentobarbital, diazepam. Found in urine: propofol, methoxyphenol, pentobarbital, amatandine, thiopental, atropine, prednisolone, coffee. Phenothiazine derivatives, tricyclic antidepressants, cholinesterase inhibitors are not detected in blood and urine.*[125]

After six hours, his analyses showing no traces of poison, the doctors of Omsk conclude to a disorder of metabolic origin[126].

Meanwhile, in Germany, the *Cinema for Peace Foundation (CFP)*, an NGO that promotes peace and democracy (but only in certain countries[127] !), called for Navalny's admission to the Berlin Charité Hospital, and chartered a special plane, which took off from Nuremberg on Friday, August 21 at 3:00 am[128]. Thus, in the afternoon, at least one German doctor was at Navalny's bedside in Omsk, while arrangements for his transfer were made. On the evening of the 21st, after the personal intervention of Vladimir Putin, the Russian authorities gave their agreement for him to be treated in Germany, despite the judicial control that forbids him to leave the Russian territory.

---

124. "Highly toxic, but unreliable *Meduza* answers key questions about Novichok-type nerve agent poisoning," *meduza.io*, September 3, 2020.

125. Translated from Russian (https://t.me/vladivostok1978/4577).

126. Anton Zverev, "Russia first treated Navalny for suspected poisoning then U-turned: doctor," *Reuters*, September 6, 2020.

127. Its scope covers the same countries as the *National Endowment for Democracy* (NED), which we will discuss below.

128. "Germany activists say they are sending plane to pick up Navalny," *Reuters*, August 20, 2020.

Those close to Navalny see this as a delaying tactic. *Liberation* insinuates that the Russian doctors are under the orders of the security services with *"the wish not to provide him with quality medical assistance and to wait until the traces of poison disappear"*[129]. On *Euronews*, a few hours before Navalny flew to Germany, the opponent Konstantin Jankauskas says that Navalny *"is kept prisoner for several days, the time to hide the substance that was used to poison him, so that the poison comes out of his blood and the investigation goes nowhere"*[130].

In an interview conducted by the *Montaigne* Institute on September 18, the economist Sergei Guriev, in addition to numerous factual errors, states:

> *Everything suggests that there was a miscalculation on the part of Moscow: it can be assumed that the plan was to suppress Navalny and then bury him in Moscow, and then to refuse to transfer the biological tests abroad while denying the poisoning. [...]*
> *It is likely that the authorities waited until the poison had stopped leaving traces in Navalny's body before letting him go. They must have thought that two days would be enough to erase all traces of it.*[131]

But not only are these accusations purely speculative, they are factually false. On September 3, on the Russian opposition media *Meduza*, an OPCW expert had already cast doubt on these specu-

129. Tatiana Serova, "Alexei Navalny still in a coma, prisoner of the Omsk hospital," *liberation.fr*, August 21, 2020.
130. "Poison is part of Putin's policy," *Euronews*, August 21, 2020.
131. "The mysterious Navalny case - Sergei Guriev's opinion," *institutmontaigne.org*, September 18, 2020.

4. The case

lations, explaining that the AChE inhibitors of nerve agents bind to cholinesterase and thus remain in the body for more than three to four weeks[132].

If the Russian secret services have the virtuosity in the use of poisons that is attributed to them, they should know it. Moreover, if Guriev had been telling the truth, this would not explain why the French, Swedish and OPCW experts (mandated by the German government) did not take their samples until between September 2 and 6, that is to say more than ten days later! Were they therefore "in cahoots" with the "FSB killers" and waiting for the traces of Novitchok to disappear? Obviously not! Conclusion: by keeping Navalny forty-eight hours, the Russian doctors did not try to hide anything, contrary to what the partisans of the conspiracy theory affirm.

On December 12, the *Times*[133] of London, followed by the *New York Post*[134] and *DW*[135], claimed that Navalny had been subjected to a second poisoning attempt *"by the Kremlin"* in the Omsk hospital before his departure for Germany, thus accusing Russian doctors of complicity. In fact, this accusation is only possible because one detail is hidden: the presence of German doctors. In its report published in *The Lancet* on 22 December, the Charité hospital revealed that Navalny had a German doctor by his side in Omsk, thirty-one hours after the onset of his symptoms - that is, from the

---

132. "There are better poisons if you really want to kill someone" The chemical weapons expert who led the OPCW's mission to Salisbury after the Novichok attack on the Skripals explains Alexey Navalny's situation, *meduza.io*, 3 September 2020.
133. Matthew Campbell, "Revealed: Kremlin made a second attempt to poison Alexei Navalny in botched assassination," *The Times*, December 12, 2020.
134. Lee Brown, "Kremlin critic Alexei Navalny reportedly survived second poisoning," *New York Post*, December 13, 2020.
135. Alex Berry, "Navalny poisoning: Russia made second assassination attempt - report," *dw.com*, December 13, 2020.

afternoon of Friday 21 August - and that by the time he was transported to Germany *"his condition had improved slightly"*[136]. Thus, the German doctors' report is clear: their Russian colleagues not only stabilized Navalny, but their treatment was effective. To claim that the Russian doctors had *"the wish not to provide him with quality medical assistance"*[137] is dishonest and lacks any journalistic ethics. Navalny's relatives and our media have lied (once again): this "second attempt" to poison him probably never happened...

On August 22, at 8 a.m., the plane left for Berlin with Navalny on board. The flight to Germany was conducted under conditions that are still unclear. While Navalny is supposed to have been poisoned by a powerful neurotoxicant, neither the flight personnel, nor the medical teams, nor the accompanying persons are subject to any particular protection measures, as the government's answers to the German parliamentarians[138] will later reveal.

Here we see the mechanisms of conspiracy: creating a narrative from disparate elements (here: symptoms of poisoning, "slowness" in evacuating Navalny to Germany, collusion between doctors and the FSB, etc.), which are linked by a "logic" (here: the government seeks to eliminate Navalny), while discarding information that disturbs (here: the characteristics of the nerve agents, the presence of the German doctors, etc.) This is the QAnon method, institutionalized and used against Russia.

---

136. See Appendix 1.

137. Tatiana Serova, *op. cit.*

138. *Antwort der Bundesregierung auf die Kleine Anfrage der Abgeordneten Dr. Anton Friesen, Armin-Paulus Hampel, Dr. Roland Hartwig, weiterer Abgeordneter und der Fraktion der AfD- Drucksache 19/23352 - Offene Fragen bezüglich des mutmaßlichen Anschlags auf Alexej Nawalny*, Deutscher Bundestag, Drucksache 19/24493, November 19, 2020 (questions 4, 6 and 69).

4.3. The telephone conversation with an "FSB agent"

On December 21, a video made the buzz, which shows Navalny phoning one of the FSB agents who would have taken part in this "poisoning" attempt[139]. Conspiracy theorists will claim that after this conversation "there is *no more doubt*"[140].

However, what does this video really tell us? According to the *Bellingcat* website, Navalny's interlocutor is an FSB agent named Konstantin Kudryavtsev, but there is no evidence that this person is really an FSB agent.

Bellingcat has explained its methodology, but it is technically far from reliable and morally questionable. In fact, instead of starting with the crime and tracing it back to the perpetrator (as a Sherlock Holmes would do), *Bellingcat* looks for individuals who best fit the hypothetical course of the crime. In practical terms, a profile of the perpetrators is established based on an imagined scenario, and then we look for the individuals who have the highest probability of matching it. Thus, we arrive at the result by a succession of approximations: we have the probability of the probability of the probability, etc., that what we find is true. To simplify: one selects facts from the conclusions, whereas the facts should lead to conclusions. This is a method that police departments try to avoid, because it leads to miscarriages of justice.

Such a methodology could be used if all the elements of the crime were known exactly in advance. The problem is that here there are many details that show that *Bellingcat does* not know how the

---

139. *Video* "Я позвонил своему убийце. Он признался," Алексей Навальный/YouTube, 21 December 2020 (https://www.youtube.com/watch?v=ibqiet6Bg38)
140. Pascal Boniface, in the program "C dans l'air" of January 28, 2021, ("Poutine / Navalny : espion, poison et corruption #cdanslair 28.01.2021", *France 5/YouTube*, January 29, 2021) (55'39").

Russian security services function or how they are structured, or even how the crime was committed and under what circumstances. Therefore, the probability that *Bellingcat* arrived at the right result is extremely low. Moreover, the American channel *CNN* - which investigated on the spot - admits that it has *"not been able"* to confirm Navalny's accusations... [141]

Furthermore, assuming that Navalny's interlocutor was indeed a member of a "poisoning" team, would he speak freely with an unknown person, on an unencrypted phone, and give details of an operation that would presumably be highly classified? Assuming that this "agent" was involved in Navalny's surveillance for four years, would he not have recognized his voice on the phone? With a large number of contradictions and errors in the functioning of the services, we have reason to believe that Navalny's interlocutor was not the one presented to us.

That said, in many countries - including France[142] - opposition movements (and even former presidents of the Republic!) are subject to special surveillance, and Russia is certainly no exception in this regard. This surveillance is probably all the more assiduous as Navalny's movement is supported and financed by foreign countries. In the United States, in 2018, it was for the same reasons that the FBI arrested Maria Butina, a young Russian woman who was - naively - seeking to bring the United States and Russia closer together. Considered a spy and foreign agent by the United States

---

141. "CNN investigation uncovers tailing of Alexey Navalny prior to poisoning," CNN, YouTube video, December 14, 2020 (08'27") (youtube.com/watch?v=n74UMp2Kmp4).
142. "France. New surveillance law seriously undermines human rights," *amnesty.org*, July 24, 2015.

4. The case

and our media, such as *Le Monde*[143] or *L'Express*[144], she would eventually be deported to her country at the request of the Kremlin. Ironically, she was politically active in Russia, in Alexeï Navalny's party[145] ! Moreover, very few media will point out that she visited Navalny in prison in April 2021[146] !

Opposition media outlet *Meduza* asked four lawyers whether Navalny's video constitutes evidence that the FSB tried to poison him. All agreed that even if it is legally possible to present the video in a trial, its content is open to manipulation and is very insufficient to prove anything[147].

As for *Bellingcat* - which is regularly referred to by far-right conspiracists, *Conspiracy Watch*, and many Western media outlets - an internal UK *Integrity Initiative* document from June 2018 on countering Russian disinformation judges it as follows:

> *Bellingcat has been somewhat discredited, both by spreading misinformation itself and by being willing to produce reports for anyone willing to pay.*[148]

This telephone conversation is therefore not credible in form. But it is not credible either in its substance. Assuming that it is a case of Novitchok poisoning, and even that the poison is of Russian

143. AFP, "United States: Russian spy Maria Butina sentenced to eighteen months in prison," *Le Monde*, April 26, 2019 (updated April 27, 2019).
144. Lucas Godignon, "Les deux vies de Maria Butina, étudiante et espionne russe," *lexpress.fr*, July 18, 2018 (updated July 19, 2018).
145. Maria Butina is among the seven candidates worth supporting according to the article "Давайте проголосуем, раз уж можно голосовать" ("Let's vote now that we're allowed to"), *navalny.com*, 6 May 2014.
146. Kahina Sekkai, "Russian ex-spy Maria Butina surprised Alexei Navalny in prison," *Paris Match*, April 2, 2021.
147. Kristina Safonova, "Indirect confessions We asked lawyers if Navalny's recording is valid proof that the FSB tried to poison him," *meduza.io*, 21 December 2020.
148. *Upskilling to Upscale: Unleashing the Capacity of Civil Society to Counter Disinformation*, Final Report, June 2018, p. 72.

origin, nothing at this stage - not even Navalny's conversation - can link the Russian authorities to this attempt. Moreover, as we shall see, the various reports on this poisoning, published by the Charité hospital, by the OPCW, by Germany, Sweden or France, are based on biomedical samples (blood and urine samples), and none of them confirms the mode of poisoning, nor does it refer to the bottles or underwear. This was confirmed by the German government in its answers to the parliamentarians[149].

4.4. The result of the analyses

There is little evidence to judge the relevance of the Western accusations of 2018 and 2020. The analyses carried out by the German, French and Swedish military laboratories[150], in September 2020, remain classified and have not been published or communicated to Russia, despite its requests. On the other hand, the data collected by the doctors who treated Navalny in Omsk and Berlin[151], the declassified version of the OPCW report[152] and - to a certain extent - the answers of the German government of 19 November 2020 and 15 February 2021, to the questions of the Bundestag parliamentarians, are available.

The analyses of military laboratories tend to affirm the presence of Novitchok, but their content is unverifiable. The observations of civilian doctors tend to contradict their conclusions, while the

---

149. *Antwort der Bundesregierung auf die Kleine Anfrage der Abgeordneten Dr. Anton Friesen, Armin-Paulus Hampel, Dr. Roland Hartwig, weiterer Abgeordneter und der Fraktion der AfD- Drucksache 19/25516*, Deutscher Bundestag, Drucksache 19/26684, February 15, 2021 (answers to questions 19 to 24).
150. See Appendix 4.
151. See appendices 1 and 2.
152. See Appendix 3.

official responses seem much less categorical than the media and hide behind military secrecy when the facts seem to contradict the statements.

On August 24, the hospital of Charity declares in a press release that the clinical analyses *"indicate intoxication by a substance of the cholinesterase inhibitor group"*[153]. However, the doctors in Omsk did not detect any. So: conspiracy? No, not necessarily. As the opposition media *Meduza* explains, the German doctors were looking for evidence of poisoning, while the Russian doctors were looking for the cause of Navalny's illness[154]. Since they were not looking for the same thing, they got different results, but they are not inconsistent.

The German government mandates the *Institut für Pharmakologie und Toxikologie der Bundeswehr* (IPTB) to carry out toxicological analyses of the samples (*Bioproben*) taken from Navalny (i.e. blood and urine). In its September 2 press release, the government states that the IPTB's analyses provided *"irrefutable proof of a chemical nerve agent of the Novitchok group"*[155].

On 14 September, Germany stated that *"the results of analyses by specialized laboratories in France and Sweden are now available and confirm the German evidence"*[156], and that it had requested the assistance of the OPCW. It reiterates its request for clarification from Russia, but does not assert or suggest that Russia may have been behind the poisoning attempt.

---

153. "Press release - Statement by Charity: Clinical findings indicate Alexei Navalny was poisoned", *charite.de*, 24 August 2020.

154. "Highly toxic, but unreliable *Meduza* answers key questions about Novichok-type nerve agent poisoning," *meduza.io*, September 3, 2020.

155. "Erklärung der Bundesregierung im Fall Nawalny" ("Statement of the Federal Government on the Nawalny Case"), Pressemitteilung 306, *Presse- und Informationsamt der Bundesregierung* (BPA), September 2, 2020.

156. "Erklärung der Bundesregierung im Fall Nawalny" ("Statement of the Federal Government on the Nawalny Case"), Pressemitteilung 322, *Presse- und Informationsamt der Bundesregierung* (BPA), September 14, 2020.

The Navalny case

It should be noted here that Germany requested the assistance of the OPCW by invoking Article VIII (paragraph 38) of the *Chemical Weapons Convention* (which does not require the sharing of data), instead of Article IX (paragraphs 3 and 4), which requires the sharing of information between the parties concerned. The German authorities refused to share information with Russia on the pretext that Navalny had been treated in Omsk and that - therefore - the Russian authorities had the results of the analyses[157]... A way of accusing without possible contradiction.

On October 6, the OPCW published its report and observed:

> *The cholinesterase inhibitor biomarkers found in Mr. Navalny's blood and urine samples have structural characteristics similar to those of toxic chemicals in Schedules 1.A.14 and 1.A.15, which were added to the Convention's Annex on Chemicals at the twenty-fourth session of the Conference of the States Parties in November 2019. This cholinesterase inhibitor is not listed in the Convention's Annex on Chemicals.* [158]

The report concludes that Navalny *"was exposed to a toxic chemical acting as a cholinesterase inhibitor."* The biomarker is named in the classified version of the report, but not the AChE inhibitor, which is not on the OPCW's list of products considered chemical weapons. Thus, contrary to Galia Ackerman's assertion in the January 28

---

157. Florian Rötzer, "Bundesregierung erklärt, zwei unabhängige Militärlabors hätten den Nowitschok-Nachweis des Bundeswehrlabors bestätigt," *heise.de*, 15 September 2020.
158. "Summary of the Report on Activities Carried out in Support of a Request for Technical Assistance by Germany (Technical Assistance Visit - TAV/01/20)," Note By The Technical Secretariat, OPCW, October 6, 2020 (S/1906/2020). See Annex 4.

4. The case

edition of "*C dans l'air*", the OPCW has not confirmed that Novitchok was involved, but only the presence of similar biomarkers[159].

In October 2020, the Swedes communicate the result of their analysis, and note[160] :

The presence of XXXX was confirmed in the patient's blood.[161]

The name of the substance is masked and obviously covered by military secrecy. So we don't know anything about it, but we can imagine that if it was Novitchok (which the Western countries expected), there would have been no reason to hide it... On January 14, 2021, the Swedish government refuses to declassify this result in order "*not to harm relations between Sweden and a foreign power*", without specifying whether it was Germany or the United States. So we don't know anything about it. But we do know that Sweden is a country where honor is a fiction subordinated to political interest: in the Julian Assange affair, the Swedish government literally "*fabricated*" accusations of rape, according to Nils Melzer, the United Nations Special Rapporteur on Torture[162].

One might think that we are trying to fight Russian opacity with Western transparency, but this does not seem to be the case...

In its statement of October 6, 2020, after the analyses of the OPCW, France and Sweden, the German government expresses firmly that there was poisoning, but is still not able to attribute responsibility to Russia:

---

159. Galia Ackerman, in the program "C dans l'air" of January 28, 2021, ("Poutine / Navalny : espion, poison et corruption #cdanslair 28.01.2021 ", France 5/YouTube, January 29, 2021) (04'30").
160. twitter.com/mazzenilsson/status/1314600936497704960
161. See Appendix 4.
162. Daniel Ryser, Yves Bachmann, Charles Hawley, "A murderous system is being created before our very eyes," *republik.ch*, January 31, 2020.

This once again unequivocally confirms the evidence that Alexei Navalny was the victim of an attack with a chemical nerve agent of the Novitchok group. This publicly unknown nerve agent has not yet been officially listed by the OPCW.

Curiously enough, in the same press release, the German government indicates that it is reluctant to register these substances with the OPCW:

The federal government is currently reviewing the detailed technical analysis report that the OPCW presented to it yesterday. Proliferation risk assessment plays a key role in the dissemination or publication of information, as well as in the question of its official categorization. Knowledge about the hazardous substance must not fall into the wrong hands.[163]

It is therefore a product not listed by the OPCW, which has "*structural similarities with the substances of the Novitchok group*"[164], but which the German government is not ready to have banned by the OPCW. It confirms its intention in its reply of 15 February 2021 to German parliamentarians who questioned it about the relevance of this decision. Without mentioning the presence of Novitchok anywhere, he states:

The nerve agent found in Alexei Navalny's house is a military agent. As with all chemical weapons, its production and use are already fundamentally prohibited by the Chemical

---

163. "Erklärung der Bundesregierung im Fall Nawalny" ("Statement of the Federal Government on the Nawalny Case"), Pressemitteilung 356, *Presse- und Informationsamt der Bundesregierung* (BPA), 6 October 2020.
164. "Erklärungen des Auswärtigen Amts in der Regierungspressekonferenz vom 07.10.2020" ("Statement by the Federal Foreign Office at the Government Press Conference on 7 October 2020"), 8 October 2020 (www.auswaertiges-amt.de/de/newsroom/regierungspressekonferenz/2403102).

Weapons Convention (CWC). The publication of the chemical formula of the nerve agent on the [OPCW] list carries considerable proliferation risks. Therefore, the federal government does not support listing the substance with the OPCW.[165]

In other words, the toxic substance found in Navalny's house would be so dangerous that banning it could present a proliferation risk greater than its danger! Moreover, if this substance originated in a *"sufficiently sophisticated"* laboratory in Russia, it is not clear why its existence should be covered by military secrecy to the point of not being able to prohibit it! Magritte would have said: *"This is not Novitchok"*!

The report of the German doctors, published on December 22, 2020, in the medical journal *The Lancet*, clearly states that they were not able to identify the presence of Novitchok when Navalny arrived, but only *"cholinesterase inhibitors"*. They state that the identification of Novitchok required further analysis by the IPTB.

But the analyses carried out by the Charity Hospital upon Navalny's arrival speak for themselves. They are the subject of an annex to the *Lancet* article[166]. An appendix that *no* mainstream media has published, reported or analyzed! Even the communication published on December 30 by Agnès Callamard and Irene Khan, special rapporteurs of the United Nations, does not mention this appendix, even

---

165. *"Antwort der Bundesregierung auf die Kleine Anfrage der Abgeordneten Dr. Anton Friesen, Armin-Paulus Hampel, Dr. Roland Hartwig, weiterer Abgeordneter und der Fraktion der AfD- Drucksache 19/25516"*, ("Response of the Federal Government to the small question of the Members of Parliament Dr. Anton Friesen, Armin-Paulus Hampel, Dr. Roland Hartwig, weiterer *Abgeordneter und der Fraktion der AfD- Drucksache 19/25516")* *Deutscher Bundestag* Anton Friesen, Armin-Paulus Hampel, Dr. Roland Hartwig, weiterer Abgeordneter und der Fraktion der AfD- Drucksache 19/25516) Deutscher Bundestag, Drucksache 19/26684, 15 February 2021.
166. See Appendix 2.

though it contains the only scientific observations available[167]. One has the right to question their competence, as well as the impartiality and integrity required by their office, when, on the other hand, they judge that the report of the American intelligence services on the assassination of Jamal Khashoggi *"provides only circumstantial evidence"* (which is true)[168].

In fact, the *Lancet* report is so little quoted because the German doctors question the military version of events. The informed reader can consult these values in the appendix of this book[169] and draw his own conclusions. A superficial research on these different results allows - with all reserve - some observations, as an indication:

- the albumin value suggests a liver problem;
- the high value of lactate dehydrogenase (LDH) suggests metabolic disorders often observed with cancerous tumors;
- the values of amylase and lipase suggest pancreatitis, which has been mentioned about Navalny in the past;
- values for C-reactive protein, leukocytes, neutrophils and erythrocytes suggest a bacterial infection;
- Amantadine is a drug often used in the treatment of Parkinson's disease;
- Lithium is used in psychiatry for the treatment of bipolar disorder and depression;
- the low butyrylcholinesterase (BChE) value-0.42 at arrival in Berlin and 0.41 at day 3-suggests exposure to a cholinesterase inhibitor, and could be explained by lithium[170];

167. spcommreports.ohchr.org/TMResultsBase/DownLoadPublicCommunication-File?gId=25830
168. "Russia responsible for Navalny poisoning, rights experts say," *un.org*, 1st March 2021.
169. See Annex 2, Appendix S2.
170. Sin J. Choi, Robert M. Derman, "Lithium and cholinesterase," *Progress in Neuro-Psychopharmacology*, Vol. 4, No. 1, 1980, pp. 107-109 (DOI: 10.1016/0364-7722(80)90067-3).

4. The case

- There are anxiolytics with anticonvulsant effects, such as diazepam and nordazepam, as well as oxazepam, used to treat behavioural disorders and anxiety. The effects of oxazepam, especially when taken in high doses with alcohol, can cause abdominal and muscle cramps, seizures and depression. These drugs are usually taken by mouth.

The presence of cholinesterase inhibitors could therefore simply be explained by the drugs ingested by Navalny himself, in all likelihood in combination with alcohol. This would explain why his symptoms were completely different from those of Sergei and Yulia Skripal in 2018, who are claimed to be victims of the same poison.

Moreover, the German doctors' report reveals that when the French, the Swedes and the OPCW took their samples - a fortnight after Navalny's arrival in Germany - his cholinesterase level was close to normal. At this stage, these laboratories were only able to detect "*cholinesterase inhibitors*", but not the substances found in Charité a few days earlier, such as lithium or drugs, which would have favored their appearance. In the absence of published results, we do not know exactly what the military found, but it is likely that, having no other explanation for the presence of these inhibitors, they were led to conclude that it was Novitchok.

By keeping their results secret, these laboratories probably did not foresee that the German doctors would publish the results of their analyses. Thanks to the latter, the hypothesis that Navalny was the victim of accidental poisoning appears more likely than a deliberate poisoning.

Navalny must obviously have known this, as he must have known that these results were going to be published; and it was probably to disqualify their conclusions that, the day before the *Lancet* article was published, Navalny posted his telephone conversation with an "FSB agent" online.

Moreover, on September 23, 2020, after his release from the Berlin hospital, on his Instagram account, Navalny warmly thanks for his *"incredible work"*[171] Dr. Kai-Uwe Eckhart, who is a specialist in nephrology and internal medicine (not toxicology!).

None of this makes it possible to draw definitive conclusions either way, but it does tend to show that the accusations made against Russia are circumstantial and not factual. This seriously puts into perspective the categorical assertions of our European parliamentarians, experts on television or *Conspiracy Watch*[172].

4.5. The film Putin's *Palace*

After his release from the Berlin hospital, Navalny did not return immediately to Russia, as he was in Kirchzarten[173], at *Black Forest Studios*[174], to make a propaganda film: *Putin's Palace*. The studios had been contacted in early December by an undisclosed California-based firm to see if they had the capacity to produce the film. This firm financed the booking of the studios and the making of the film in Germany[175].

Obviously, the film is already partially made; some scenes with Navalny are still missing, which are shot in December 2020. On

---

171. https://www.facebook.com/navalny/photos/a.368739553145134/3670231166329273/?-type=3
172. Antoine Hasday, *op. cit.*
173. Alexei Makartsev, Georg Rudiger, "Nawalny produzierte Putin-Film im Schwarzwald" ("Navalny produced a film about Putin in the Black Forest"), *Badische Neueste Nachrichten*, 23 January 2021.
174. www.blackforest-studios.com/
175. Ralf Deckert, "Palast-Video in Blackforest Studios produziert" ("The palace video produced at Black Forest Studios"), *schwarzwaelder-bote.de*, 22 January 2021.

January 19, 2021, it was broadcast by all the Western media and viewed several tens of millions of times. It is about a sumptuous "palace" located in Gelendjik, which a rumor - maintained by his opponents - attributes the property to Vladimir Putin.

In fact, this is a warmed-over accusation, purely speculative and which strictly speaking no element confirms. This controversy began in 2010 with a letter from a certain Sergei Kolesnikov to President Medvedev, in which he accused Vladimir Putin, then Prime Minister, of having built a palace for himself with corruption money. But without providing any proof of his allegations, as noted by the *Financial Times*[176]. Today, of course, attempts are being made to pass Kolesnikov off as a "whistleblower" who, after his letter, "*went abroad, of course*" to escape Putin's vindictiveness[177]. In reality, the opposite happened: after legal proceedings were opened against him for embezzlement and fraud, Kolesnikov left Russia by stealth in September 2010[178], to settle in the United States. It was then, in December 2010, that he wrote his letter accusing Vladimir Putin[179]. Everything suggests that this letter is more the product of a spirit of vengeance than the manifestation of a concern for justice.

What is known about the "palace" tends to confirm that it is a very high standard hotel complex, with a financing structure involving several investors. The owner of this monumental construction would have been the Russian billionaire Alexander Ponomarenko,

---

176. Catherine Belton, "A realm fit for a tsar," *Financial Times*, November 30, 2011.

177. Galia Ackerman, in the program " C dans l'air " of January 28, 2021, (" Poutine / Navalny : espion, poison et corruption #cdanslair 28.01.2021 ", *France 5/Youtube*, January 29, 2021) (20'30").

178. Catherine Belton, *op. cit.*

179. www.miamioh.edu/cas/_files/documents/havighurst/kolesnikov-medvedev-letters/letter-to-medvedev-engtrans.pdf

and is currently Arkadi Rotenberg[180]. The total cost of the real estate complex would be one hundred billion rubles (about 1.11 billion euros), which is less than the *Bellagio* Hotel in Las Vegas[181] and other[182]. It is this financing structure with multiple stakeholders that explains the delays in the project, which was initiated before 2010 and is still not completed. By comparison, considerably larger projects, such as the Kerch Bridge or the restoration of the Constantine Palace near St. Petersburg, carried out under Putin, were completed in three to four years.

Navalny's film shows luxury furniture, including a coffee table costing 4.3 million rubles, a vase costing 2.6 million and a toilet brush costing 62,000 rubles[183], etc., which do not exist! The images of *"indelicate workers who wallowed in Putin's sofas"* mentioned by Galia Ackerman[184] on *France 5* are montages: in fact, they are synthetic images. The photos showing Putin in "his" swimming pool are photomontages, because everything is still in the state of rough work[185]. As a Russian Internet user who visited the construction site demonstrated, the building is still under construction[186] ! The icing on the cake is that the eagle seen on the portal of "Putin's palace" is not the Russian eagle, but the Montenegrin one[187] ! The analysis

180. AFP, "Russie : un milliardaire assure être le propriétaire du "palais de Poutine" ", *lematin.ch*, 30 January 2021.
181. Wikipedia article "Bellagio (resort)".
182. "Top 10: most expensive hotels ever built," *The Luxury Travel Expert*, March 9, 2020.
183. Program "C dans l'air" of February 3, 2021, ("Can Navalny bring down Putin? #cdanslair 03.02. 2020 ", *France 5/YouTube*, February 4, 2021) (36'18").
184. Galia Ackerman, in the program "C dans l'air" of January 28, 2021, ("Poutine / Navalny : espion, poison et corruption #cdanslair 28.01.2021 ", *France 5/Youtube*, January 29, 2021) (20'58").
185. mobile.twitter.com/27khv/status/1354130071381020673
186. Mash Video, "Сказочный дворец: первая экскурсия по дворцу в Геленджике" ("A Fairy Tale Palace: First Excursion to Gelendjik Palace"), YouTube video, January 29, 2021 (https://www.youtube.com/watch?v=vBcWdHe8j_g)
187. twitter.com/ValLisitsa/status/1355235937303879680

4. The case

of the 3D modeling work done by *Luminous Labs* shows that it is a considerable work and a cost probably far beyond the capabilities of Navalny's team[188]... An example of disinformation!

Moreover, a careful ear will notice that Navalny does not use the language usually spoken in Russia: it is peppered with anglicisms, turns of phrase and expressions that clearly have an English origin. It is therefore very likely that Navalny only had to read a script written for him by the team from Los Angeles...

On France 5, Le *Monde*'s correspondent in Moscow sees the no-fly zone *"just above the property"* as proof that the "palace" does belong to Vladimir Putin[189]. This is also disinformation.

In fact, the "palace" is located in a border area adjacent to NATO, where tension has increased since 2008 (Georgia), 2014 (Ukraine and Crimea) and 2015 (war in Syria)[190]. Gelendjik is located on the Black Sea, not far from the Russian-Georgian border and about 40 kilometers from the Novorossiisk naval base. Not only is this base home to part of the *Black Sea Fleet*, the main elements of the 7th airborne division[191] and an air defense regiment[192], but it is also the main logistics base[193] for the Russian contingent deployed in Syria. In addition, about 50 kilometers behind the "palace" site is the 10th special forces brigade (*spetsnaz*) (see Figure 1).

---

188. Lunimous Labs, "ARCH-VIZ ARTST Reviews Rendering of PUTIN's PALACE!", You-Tube video, February 18, 2021 (https://www.youtube.com/watch?v=FOWMgLre7j0).
189. Benoît Vitkine in the program "C dans l'air" of January 28, 2021, ("Poutine / Navalny : espion, poison et corruption #cdanslair 28.01.2021 ", *France 5/Youtube*, January 29, 2021) (58'10").
190. Steven Horrell, "A NATO Strategy for Security in the Black Sea Region," *The Atlantic Council*, October 2016.
191. fi.pinterest.com/pin/235946467958184733/
192. www.pinterest.de/pin/235946467958177288/
193. Igor Sutyagin, "Detailing Russian Forces in Syria," *Royal United Services Institute (RUSI)*, November 13, 2015.

This is why NATO is conducting intense electronic intelligence activity[194] in this area, close to Ukraine and Georgia, including RC-135V/W *Rivet Joint,* E-3A AWACS and U-2S aircraft[195]. These NATO reconnaissance flights are often decoys aimed at provoking the electronic activity of the Russian air defense in order to monitor it[196]. In April 2021 alone, no less than eighty-three reconnaissance flights were conducted by U.S. and NATO air forces in this area[197]. The airspace restrictions are therefore not limited to "Putin's palace", but concern the entire coastal and border region where electronic installations for the defense of Russia's southern flank are concentrated. But obviously, our "experts" of "C dans l'air" hide the context to create their narrative...

The information, relayed by Galia Ackerman on RTBF, that the property is guarded by the FSB is equally spurious[198]. It is a myth that stems from the arrest of a group of environmentalists by a border guard patrol in this area in 2011. Ms. Ackerman is using a misinformation technique here based on confusion. As she knows, the border guards are a separate administration from the FSB and have nothing to do with the security services: in this coastal area near Turkey and Georgia, their mission is to hunt down arms and drug smuggling.

As we can see, the broadcasting of Navalny's film is surrounded by manipulations and distortions of reality. Pseudo-experts put

---

194. David Cenciotti, "Eyes On Crimea: U.S. Intelligence Gathering Aircraft Increasingly Flying Over the Black Sea," *The Avionist*, April 6, 2018.

195. itamilradar.com

196. David Axe, "That U.S. Air Force B-52 Flying Over The Black Sea Was Bait For The Russians," *Forbes*, August 30, 2020

197. natsouth.livejournal.com/tag/black%20sea

198. D.F., "The palace that 'does not belong to Putin': how the Kremlin is trying to discredit Navalny's investigation", *rtbf.be*, 31 January 2021.

4. The case

together facts in a way that gives them a (false) coherence, in order to support prejudices and to feed a propagandist type of discourse.

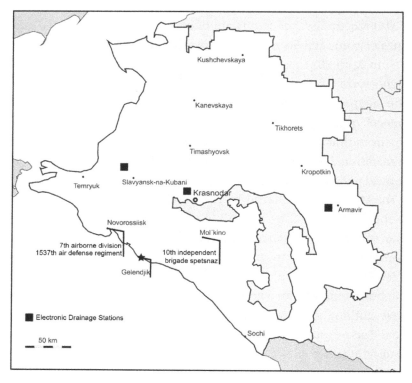

Figure 1 - Military facilities in the area near Gelendjik (where "Putin's Palace" is located) in the Krasnodar district. This area near the southern border of Russia includes a large number of early warning and early detection facilities, and the Novorossiisk naval air base. This explains the flight restrictions.

4.6. Navalny's arrest

Upon his return to Russia on January 17, 2021, the Russian authorities arrested Navalny. Western media deliberately and systematically fail to explain the reasons for this, suggesting - or even claiming - that he was arrested for his political views.

In its *"19:30"* of January 23, 2021, *Radio Télévision Suisse* (RTS) implied that he had been imprisoned for broadcasting *"revelations about a secret residence of Vladimir Putin [...] estimated to be worth one and a half billion francs"*[199] and repeated the claim on February 7 that the opponent had been *"sentenced to prison for defying the Kremlin"*[200]. This is disinformation.

In the same spirit, on February 2, President Emmanuel Macron tweeted:

> *The conviction of Alexei Navalny is unacceptable. Political disagreement is never a crime. We call for his immediate release. Respect for human rights and democratic freedom are non-negotiable.*[201]

Like his handler Donald Trump, Macron is spreading *fake news*. In fact, Navalny has not been convicted again, but his suspended sentence has been revoked. On February 4, Joe Biden, who was thought to be wiser and more thoughtful than Donald Trump, followed the same path as his predecessor in presenting his foreign policy:

> *Mr. Navalny, like all Russian citizens, is entitled to his rights under the Russian Constitution. He has been targeted for*

199. www.rts.ch/play/tv/19h30/video/19h30?urn=urn:rts:video:11919988
200. rts.ch/play/tv/redirect/detail/11956261?startTime=1866
201. twitter.com/EmmanuelMacron/status/1356676542257102853

exposing corruption. He should be released immediately and unconditionally. [202]

To say that the arrest is linked to a *"political disagreement"*, to the fact that he *"denounced corruption"*, or to say that it is *"arbitrary"*, as Jean-Yves Le Drian asserts[203] is simply a lie. But this is what is pushing the European Union to demand his immediate release[204].

A Western narrative is developing around the claim that Navalny is a *"prisoner of conscience.* The *BBC*[205] and *Swiss Television*[206] compare him to Nelson Mandela. However, on February 21, 2021, *Amnesty International* revoked Navalny's *"prisoner of conscience"* status because *"he has advocated violence and discrimination and has never withdrawn his statements"*[207]. Also, ironically, Mandela remained on the U.S. terrorist list until 2008, nine years after he was elected president of South Africa[208] !...

202. *Remarks by President Biden on America's Place in the World*, The White House, February 4, 2021.
203. *Statement by Mr. Jean-Yves Le Drian, Minister of Europe and Foreign Affairs, in response to a question on the situation in Russia by Mr. Alexei Navalny, at the National Assembly on January 26, 2021*, Vie-publique.fr, January 26, 2021.
204. Sam Meredith, "U.S., European officials condemn arrest of poisoned Putin critic Alexei Navalny, as calls grow for his immediate release," CNBC, January 18, 2021; "Detention Of Kremlin Critic Navalny Sparks Strong Condemnation, Demands For His Immediate Release," *RFE/RL*, January 18, 2021.
205. "Alexeï Navalny: the Nelson Mandela of Russia?", international press review, *france-culture.fr*, 19 July 2013/.
206. "Poutine-Navalny, le duel", broadcast *"Géopolitis" of 21 February 2021, RTS.ch*, 21 February 2021 (08'05").
207. Sarah Rainsford, "Amnesty strips Alexei Navalny of 'prisoner of conscience' status," *BBC News*, February 23, 2021.
208. Mark Karlin, "Nelson Mandela Was Only Removed From the US Terrorist List in 2008," *Truthout.org*, January 6, 2014.

Amnesty's decision was a cold shower for Westerners and Navalny's supporters, and the pressure to reverse it was enormous. On May 7, the NGO reversed its decision and explained[209] :

> *This means that by confirming Navalny's status as a prisoner of conscience, we are not endorsing his political agenda, but stressing the urgent need for his rights, including access to independent medical care, to be recognized and enforced by the Russian authorities.*
>
> *Alexei Navalny was not imprisoned for any recognizable crime, but for demanding the right to equal participation in public life for himself and his supporters, and for demanding a government free of corruption. These are acts of conscience and should be recognized as such.*

This decision is not the result of a reassessment of the nature of Navalny's opinions, but the simple fact of his imprisonment, the reasons for which are being adapted.

Because following his indictment in connection with the dispute with the French company *Yves Rocher*, Navalny was placed under judicial supervision, after which he was obliged to report twice a month to the Russian prison authority, until the end of his probationary period (December 30, 2020).

It is because Navalny did not comply with this obligation, that he was arrested. Naturally, it is carefully avoided to mention that Navalny has already violated this rule six times in 2020 (twice in January, once in February, March, July and August), but that the Russian authorities were then lenient. As Jean-Didier Revoin, *Swiss*

---

209. "Statement on Alexei Navalny's status as Prisoner of Conscience, *Amnesty International*, 7 May 2021.

4. The case

Television's Moscow correspondent, notes, Navalny *"has never been sentenced to a prison term, unlike many other opponents"*[210]. Thus, despite his multiple offences, and contrary to what is claimed in the West, Navalny has benefited from an unusual clemency. So much so, in fact, that some (conspiracy theorists) in Russia believe that he is being used by the Kremlin to weaken the main opposition parties.

To claim that the revocation of his suspension is political in nature, it is claimed that Navalny was physically unable to fulfill his obligations. *France 24* states that he was unable to do so *"because he was simply hospitalized in Germany"*[211]. *France 5* explains that *"he was in a coma"*[212], and *Swiss Television* that *"he was convalescing in Germany after his poisoning"*[213]. This is not true.

First, her obligation to report was suspended by the Russian authorities for the duration of her hospitalization in Berlin. On the other hand, the report of the doctors of the Charité hospital, published on December 22, 2020, attests to his discharge from the hospital on September 23, 2020[214] and the end of his symptoms on October 12, 2020[215].

After leaving the hospital, Navalny made a quick trip to Basel, Switzerland. On October 1st, he gave an interview to *Spiegel* in Germany[216]. On October 14, he flew under the protection of

210. www.rts.ch/play/tv/19h30/video/19h30?urn=urn:rts:video:11919988&start-Time=285
211. https://youtu.be/u589gXqN9ZE?t=151
212."Can Navalny bring down Putin?#cdans lair 03.02.2020," *France 5/YouTube*, February 4, 2021 (15'10").
213. Newspaper of 19:30, Télévision Suisse Romande, January 18, 202
214. "Alexei Navalny: Russian activist discharged from Berlin hospital," *BBC News*, September 23, 2020.
215. "Russia gives Kremlin critic Navalny an ultimatum: Return immediately or face jail," *Reuters*, December 28, 2020.
216. Benjamin Bidder, Christian Esch, "Es war kein Schmerz, es war etwas Schlimmeres" ("It was not pain, it was something worse"), *Der Spiegel*, 1ᵉʳ October 2020.

the *Landeskriminalamt* (LKA) of Baden-Württemberg to Ibach in southern Germany, where he spent a few days getting back into shape[217]. On November 27, he spoke in a teleconference to European parliamentarians to demand sanctions against Russia[218]. On December 28, Navalny flew to the Canary Islands for a seaside holiday, which he decided to take unexpectedly against the advice of his German bodyguards[219]. Back in Kirchzarten, he took part in the making of his film, until January 13[220], before leaving for Russia on January 17[221]. Everything seems to show that Navalny would have been able to return to Russia to fulfill his judicial obligations, and that our media have played with the facts... The Munich Charter is only a distant memory!

On December 28, the Russian prison authorities sent Navalny a warning (with a copy to his lawyer and press secretary) to report to[222], but he ignored it. Therefore, the Russian prison authorities could hardly ignore this new highly publicized offense of almost three months, and revoked his suspended sentence. Navalny was probably hoping to benefit once again from the clemency of the authorities; but with the broadcasting of his film, and his calls for sanctions against Russia, this was probably naive on his part... Because in these conditions, even if the Russian authorities had

---

217. "Sportstudent Björn machte Nawalny nach dem Giftanschlag wieder fit" (Sportstudent Björn got Navalny fit after the poisoning attempt"), *rtl.de*, February 15, 2021.

218. David M. Herszenhorn, "Navalny urges EU to sanction Russian oligarchs in Europe," *Politico.eu*, November 27, 2020.

219. "Nawalny - Krach mit den Leibwächtern" (Navalny: quarrel with his bodyguards"), *FOCUS Magazin*, 3/2021, January 23, 2021.

220. Alexei Makartsev, Georg Rudiger, *op. cit.*

221. Ralf Deckert, "Palast-Video in Blackforest Studios produziert", *schwarzwaelder-bote. de*, 22 January 2021

222. "Press release on Russian-German contacts on the "Alexey Navalny case," *Russian Foreign Ministry*, 1st February 2021.

4. The case

wanted to show - once again - leniency towards him, this would have been incomprehensible for the Russian public opinion.

Navalny did not really *"jump into the lion's den"*. Two factors may have played a role in his decision.

The first is that he was probably misled by the European elites he met in Germany, who were convinced that he represented a majority current in Russia. Thus, Pascal Boniface says: *"When you see the luxury of precautions they take to prevent him from speaking, well, you see that he is not without influence."*[223] However, after his arrest on January 17, in fact of *"luxury of precautions"*, the police let him have his cell phone, with which he filmed himself in the police station[224]. In fact, by taking their desires for realities, the Westerners led Navalny to overestimate the mobilization in Russia upon his return, and are probably - paradoxically - at the origin of the failure of their own strategy, as we shall see.

The second is that he could not really avoid returning to Russia, because politically that is his "raison d'être": already not very famous in Russia, he would lose a large part of his support by staying abroad. One could even imagine that, if the Russian "power" had really wanted to get rid of him, it would have been enough not to let him return to Russia, or even to deprive him of his nationality...

After his sentence was confirmed, Navalny was taken to Moscow's SIZO-1 detention prison[225], and then transferred in February to the penal colony No. 2 (FKU No. 2) in Pokrov, east of Moscow[226].

---

223. Pascal Boniface, video "Alexeï Navalny: imprisoned but not gagged", *YouTube*, 25 January 2021 (03'00").

224. Dpa/AFP, "Navalny decries 'mockery of justice' at rushed hearing," *dw.com*, January 18, 2021.

225. fsin-atlas.ru/catalog/object/matrosska/

226. Alexei Ivanov, "Навальный найден в Петушинском районе Владимирской области" ("Navalny is in the Vladimir region, in the Petushinski raion"), *zavtra.ru*, February 27, 2021.

5. Perceptions and consequences of the case in Russia

5.1. Poisoning

The announcement that Navalny had been poisoned quickly and massively mobilized the media. Westerners rejoiced at this incident, which confirmed their prejudices about Vladimir Putin, and European parliamentarians retained only one possible cause for Navalny's discomfort: an assassination attempt, despite the fact that Germany did *not* formally declare it.

In Russia, on the other hand, where the government is said to be hated by its population, public opinion has questioned the incident itself and the Western readiness to condemn Russia. With good sense, it saw several possible causes. As the *Levada Center*'s investigation, conducted immediately after Navalny's telephone conversation with an "FSB agent", shows (see Table 3).

Perception of the possible causes of Navalny's poisoning

There was no poisoning, it was staged	30 %
It is a provocation of the Western special services	19 %
This is an attempt by the authorities to eliminate a political opponent	15 %
It is a personal revenge of people involved in his investigations	7 %
It is a struggle within the Russian opposition	6 %
Health problems, accidental poisoning, common poisoning	1 %
Other	4 %
It is difficult to answer	19 %

Table 3 - Survey conducted by the Levada Center on the perception of Navalny's poisoning in Russia. [Source: "Отравление Алексея Навального" ("Alexei Navalny's poisoning"), levada.ru, December 24, 2020.]

As can be seen, only 15 percent of Russians consider that it could be an attempt to eliminate the Russian government, while 67 percent see another cause. The increasing number of attacks on Russia by European politicians, such as Donald Trump or Emmanuel Macron, has created a background noise that discredits the attacks themselves and demobilizes Russian citizens. This phenomenon goes even further: Navalny is considered by many as a puppet of the West, even as a traitor, and his speech is simply not listened to. So we are witnessing an asymmetrical phenomenon: the more the West tries to promote Navalny, the less credible he is.

This explains why the perception of the Navalny affair there is the opposite of what the Western media present to us. For example, polls conducted by the independent institute VTsIOM at the end of August 2020 - *after* the "poisoning" attempt - show a slight increase in approval of President Putin's action (see Table 4 and Table 5).

Approval of the action of the Russian government and Vladimir Putin

	22-28.06.20	29.06-05.07.20	06-12.07.20	13-19.07.20	20-26.07.20	27.07-02.08.20	03-09.08.20	10-16.08.20	17-23.08.20	24-30.08.20
President of Russia	64,9	64,2	63,6	61,2	61,5	60	60,3	60,5	61,9	62,3
Head of Government of Russia	39,4	40	38,8	39	41,5	41,1	40,8	40,4	43,9	42,6
Government of Russia	38,4	38,4	36,2	36,4	37	36,8	35,5	34	36,9	36,3

Table 4 - Responses to the question "Do you approve of the action of...
[Russian president, Russian prime minister, Russian government]?"
We see that the media coverage of Navalny's "poisoning" had no effect,
and that Putin's approval actually increased.
[Source: Рейтинги доверия политикам, оценки работы президента и
правительства, подержка политических партий (Trust in politicians, evaluation
of the president and the government's performance, support for political parties),
wciom.ru, September 4, 2020]

In early 2021, the *Levada Center* observes a slight uptick in Navalny's popularity from 2% in November 2020 to 5% in January 2021, while Putin's approval drops from 65% to 64%. But in February, Navalny drops to 4% and Putin rises to 65%. By comparison, Emmanuel Macron then has only 36% positive views[227]. Thus, Western efforts to portray Russia as a totalitarian state are met with much broader popular support for the government than in France.

---

227. Grégoire Poussielgue, "Macron makes a breakthrough among young people," *lesechos.fr*, February 4, 2021 (updated February 5, 2021).

5. Perceptions and consequences of the case in Russia

Approval of the action of Vladimir Putin

	August 2020	Sept. 2020	Oct. 2020	Nov. 2020	Jan. 2021	Feb. 2021
I agree	66	69	68	65	64	65
I do not approve	33	31	30	34	34	34
I can't answer	1	1	1	1	2	2

Table 5 - Approval of Vladimir Putin's action (in %). [Source: "The approval of institutions and trust to politicians," Levada Center, February 26, 2021].

5.2. Reception of the film *Putin's Palace*

The broadcasting of the film made in Germany at the end of 2020 had a worldwide impact. Benefiting from the promotion of the Western media, it very quickly reached more than 100 million views in less than ten days. In forty-eight hours, the film had 50 million views and 17.4 million viewing hours[228]. Of course, no one has really analyzed the genesis of this astronomical number. It is therefore difficult to go into detail, but we can see *that, on average,* Internet users have only seen 18% of the film. According to the *Levada Center,* only 26% of those surveyed have seen it in Russia (see Figure 2).

These data raise questions because, obviously, a large part of these views were of very short duration. By comparison, we can observe that the video of McFly and Carlito, made at the request of Emmanuel Macron, was viewed 10 million times in two days, thanks to the intervention of bots[229]. Considering the resources involved in its production and the political importance it has been given in the West, it is

---

228. intellinews.com/navalny-s-putin-s-palace-expose-passes-50mn-views-in-two-days-his-most-popular-video-ever-201021/
229. Blast, "Macron, Mcfly, and Carlito: Disturbing facts behind the propaganda operation," *YouTube*, March 5, 2021 (https://www.youtube.com/watch?v=d4mwwFsfYvI).

reasonable to think that the same was true of Navalny's film, but in the absence of serious studies, we will leave our conclusions unresolved.

Notoriety of Alexei Navalny's film in Russia

Figure 2 - Responses to the question "Have you heard of Alexei Navalny's film Putin's Palace?" (in %). [Source: "The film 'Palace for Putin,'" Levada Center, February 8, 2021].

In fact, the perception of the film in Russia suffered from the exaggerated notoriety it received worldwide. The contrast with the deplorable image of the United States at the same time and the failure to deal with the Covid crisis in the West highlighted the "propagandistic" exploitation of the Russian opponent.

As for the perception of Vladimir Putin, we see that for the majority of respondents (77%) it remained unchanged (see Figure 3). The 17% who perceived a deterioration seem out of proportion to the media hype surrounding the film.

Image of Vladimir Putin after the release of the film Navalny

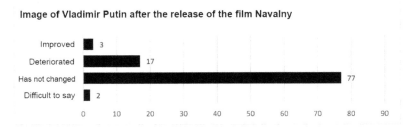

Figure 3 - Responses to the question "Did your impression of Vladimir Putin change after the film?" (in %). [Source: "The film 'Palace for Putin,'" Levada Center, February 8, 2021].

5. Perceptions and consequences of the case in Russia

5.3. Events in January 2021

The broadcasting of the film was followed, on January 23, 2021, by demonstrations in the major cities of Russia. They were shown in a loop on the Western media, which saw it as a success for Navalny. It is certainly a media coup, but to see it as a success is probably going too fast.

First, the disproportionate coverage of these protests in the Western media gave many Russians the impression that they served Western interests, and masked the protests in their own countries (for health enforcement, global security, etc.). Second, the United States vastly overestimated popular support for Navalny, as evidenced by the U.S. Embassy in Moscow publishing protest routes on January 22 to warn its citizens[230]. Third, the tweets[231] and the dissemination of messages of support[232] for the protesters by diplomatic personnel (see Annex 5) were perceived - rightly or wrongly - as a form of interference, and gave the impression that Navalny was being "steered" from outside, thus contributing to discrediting him.

Pascal Boniface saw *"brutally repressed"* demonstrations, and *"truncheons versus snowballs"*[233]. However, if the Russian demonstrators are obviously less brutal than their French counterparts, the same is true for the Russian police, who seem to have better self-control than their French colleagues. In fact, we have not seen any LBD shots in the face, nor hands torn off by disencryption grenades,

---

230. ru.usembassy.gov/demonstration-alert-u-s-mission-russia-5/
231. twitter.com/sbg1/status/1352963201168789505
232. twitter.com/Joyce_Karam/status/1353062682019028994
233. Video "Alexeï Navalny : imprisoned but not gagged", *Pascal Boniface/YouTube*, 25 January 2021 (00'55").

nor any of the eye-gouging that they try to hide in France[234], and which has earned it the distinction of being singled out by the United Nations High Commissioner for Human Rights for *"violent and excessive use of force"*[235], along with Sudan, Zimbabwe and Haiti (and not just *"as a prosperous country"*, as the newspaper *Libération* claims.[236]). In fact, the demonstrations in Russia (like those in Hong Kong and elsewhere), which are repeated on our screens, help to mask the demonstrations of the Gilets jaunes or against "global security", which have disappeared from the public media, while the broadcasting of images of police brutality[237] is suppressed... What the media call "interpellations" in France become "arrests" in Russia. Our media appear more as organs of influence than organs of information...

As for the figures of the participation in these demonstrations, the Western media had a field day: over there, as here, these figures are difficult to verify and are the object of the most diverse manipulations. According to Navalny's organization, there were 250,000 demonstrators throughout Russia. But the independent Russian media *Znak* gives probably more realistic estimates (see Table 6).

234. Frédéric Lemaire, Julien Baldassarra, "Videos of police violence: *Le Parisien* washes its face white", *acrimed.org*, 19 January 2021.
235. "High Commissioner Bachelet calls on States to take strong action against inequalities," 40th session of the UN Human Rights Council in Geneva, *ohchr.org*, 6 March 2019.
236. AFP, "Gilets jaunes : l'ONU réclame une enquête sur "l'usage excessive de la force", le gouvernement réplique ", *Libération*, 6 mars 2019.
237. Mélanie Vecchio, Clément Boutin, "Global security': opening of an investigation after the broadcasting of images of a policeman beating a demonstrator in Paris," *BFM TV*, January 30, 2021.

5. Perceptions and consequences of the case in Russia

Number of demonstrators in Russia on January 23, 2021

	Participation: independent estimate	Participation: authorities' estimate	Interpellations	Participation as % of population
Moscow	15 000	4 000	300	0,13
Saint Petersburg	10 000	-	162	0,2
Yekaterinburg	5 000	3 000	14	0,4
Novosibirsk	4 000	-	90	0,3
Vladivostok	3 000	500	35	0,5
Krasnoyarsk	3 000	-	46	0,3
Tyumen	800		3	0,12
Omsk	2 000	-	18	0,17
Irkutsk	2 000	-	6	0,3
Chelyabinsk	2 500	900	33	0,2
Barnaul	1 500	-	3	0,2
Khabarovsk	1 000	250	28	0,17
Total	49 800		738	0,25

Table 6 - Participation in the events of January 23, 2021. [Source: znak.ru]

In reality, support for Navalny is less popular than the Western media would have us believe. On *France 5*, Bernard Guetta sees a *"large-scale movement"*[238] in these demonstrations. This is not true. A survey by the *Levada Center* shows that the perception of the January 2021 demonstrators has even deteriorated compared to previous demonstrations (see Figure 4), especially those in Khabarovsk against the arrest of the governor for murder[239]. One reason for this is that the opposition associated with Navalny is

---

238. Bernard Guetta in the program "Le 5 sur 5 ! - C à Vous - 03/02/2021", *France 5/You-Tube*, February 3, 2021 (17'07").
239. AFP, "New demonstration in Russia against the arrest of the governor of Khabarovsk," *Le Monde*, 1st August 2020.

The Navalny case

far from democratic and unified: it includes disparate factions of the non-parliamentary opposition, ranging from the far right to the former Stalinist communist party[240]. As for its composition and popularity, this "opposition" is more like the Capitol Hill rioters of January 6 in Washington than the Yellow Vests.

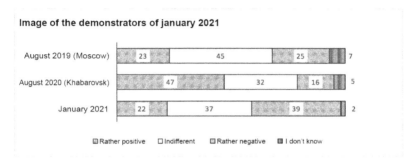

Figure 4 - - Levada Center survey of January 2021 protesters' perceptions [in %].
[Source: "January protests," Levada Center, February 11, 2021].

Moreover, the January mobilization was not really about the Navalny case, but about economic problems. Indeed, even if Russia has suffered proportionally less from the Covid crisis than Western countries, the general state of its economy is weak and is reflected in a deterioration of the standard of living. As the *Levada Center*'s survey shows (see Figure 5), this situation is creating discontent that is leading to protests unrelated to the Navalny case, to which Navalny is not providing answers.

---

240. "Дубинки вместо диалога - попрание прав народа! Заявление Московского городского комитета КПРФ" ("Clubs instead of dialogue - trampling of people's rights! Statement of the Moscow Committee of the Communist Party of the Russian Federation"), Press Service, Communist Party City Committee, Moscow, January 24, 2021.

5. Perceptions and consequences of the case in Russia

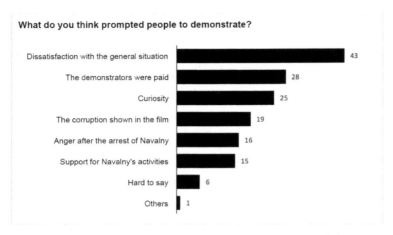

What do you think prompted people to demonstrate?

- Dissatisfaction with the general situation — 43
- The demonstrators were paid — 28
- Curiosity — 25
- The corruption shown in the film — 19
- Anger after the arrest of Navalny — 16
- Support for Navalny's activities — 15
- Hard to say — 6
- Others — 1

Figure 5 - Levada Center survey of January 2021 protesters' motivation (%). [Source: "January protests," Levada Center, February 11, 2021].

The results of the January protests were disappointing for Navalny's supporters: they expected a massive uprising of the population, but they succeeded in mobilizing only a fraction of it, including a large majority of teenagers. The Western media attributed the fading of the protests to fear of the government, but in fact the protesters met with growing public disapproval. On February 4, 2021, this led Leonid Volkov, Navalny's second-in-command, to ask his activists to stop protesting until the spring[241]. Clearly, the strategy adopted is counterproductive, but the Westerners, blinded by their own perception of the situation, are pushing in the wrong direction. As noted by *Radio Free Europe/Radio Liberty*[242], a new strategy is needed. This was discussed on February 8 in Brussels, during a meeting between representatives of the European Union

241. "Navalny's team suspends further protests until the spring, refocusing on campaign efforts ahead of Russia's fall parliamentary elections," *meduza.io*, February 4, 2021
242. "Navalny Team Switches Tactics In Call For New Protest In Russia," *Radio Free Europe/Radio Liberty*, February 9, 2021.

countries, the United States, Canada, the United Kingdom, Ukraine, as well as Leonid Volkov and Vladimir Achourkov, another Navalny collaborator[243].

This shows - if it were necessary - that there is an active work of Western interference associated with Navalny's movement. The problem is that the West's persistence in this way provokes a phenomenon similar to asymmetric conflicts: instead of provoking criticism of the government, it stimulates national sentiment and reinforces distrust of Navalny. The Western strategy is out of step with the Russian reality.

The new strategy was announced on 23 March on Navalny's website: the demonstrations would resume once 500,000 people had registered to take part[244]. A week later, Navalny went on a hunger strike, probably to catalyze the determination of his supporters. The result was a deterioration in his health. On 18 April, his entourage declared that "his life was hanging by a thread" and announced large-scale demonstrations for 21 April. At this stage, there are a little more than 466,000 registrants. Navalny was transferred to a prison hospital on 19 April, and his civilian doctors were able to visit him on 21.

In the end, we do not know the real figures of the participation in these demonstrations. *Reuters* mentions about 10,000 people in Moscow and 7,000-9,000 in St. Petersburg[245], the Ministry of the Interior obviously gives slightly lower figures, the truth probably being somewhere in between. In any case, the turnout seems to have been much lower than in January.

---

243. twitter.com/PLPermRepEU/status/1358753978750808067
244. "Как освободить Навального. Наш план" ("How to free Navalny. Our plan"), *navalny.com*, March 23, 2021.
245. Polina Ivanova, Maria Tsvetkova, Polina Nikolskaya, "Russia arrests over 1,700 at rallies for hunger-striking Navalny," *Reuters*, 22 April 2021.

5. Perceptions and consequences of the case in Russia

Demonstrations which our media give a world-wide repercussion therefore gather only a fraction of the number of participants that discontent pushes in the streets every week in France. In fact, like any other people, the Russians refuse foreign interference in their affairs, and the Western foolishness does not lead to any improvement on the spot...

5.4. Navalny's image

In fact, Navalny's "success" is also the reason why he has no real credibility in Russia: for many Russians he is a puppet of the West. The problem is that our media present us with an image that is devoid of any information that could contradict our prejudices.

On February 3, in the program "*C dans l'air*" on *France 5*, François Clémenceau said that the film has strengthened the image of Navalny[246]. The statement seems logical, but it is false. Obviously, at no point in the program does it mention the "debunking" of the film, which was put online a few days before[247]. However, this not only showed that the film was a lie, but also highlighted the considerable work of 3D modeling that it required... and that it was necessary to pay! This Western financial support[248] is perceived as a form of betrayal.

Therefore, after briefly rising three points from November 2020 to its all-time high of 5 percent, Navalny's popularity dropped back to 4

246. François Clémenceau in the program "C dans l'air" of February 3, 2021, ("Can Navalny bring down Putin? #cdanslair 03.02.2020 ", *France 5/YouTube*, February 4, 2021) (24'35")
247. video "Putin's Palace? Navalny's Exposé 'Palace' Is Just An Unfinished Hotel Project," *YouTube*, January 30, 2021 (https://www.youtube.com/watch?v=Hz3immwPJBE).
248. https://www.ned.org/region/eurasia/russia-2020/

percent in February[249]. This makes sense, as it comes from the hype on the social networks *Telegram* and *TikTok*, where the 18-24 year olds who make up the bulk of his audience are located (see Figure 7). This support itself is an optical illusion, as this is the category with the lowest political awareness and the least votes[250]. Moreover, not only has the number of people who approve of Navalny's action decreased, but those who disapprove have increased from 50% to 56%. Thus, the "success" that is presented to us in the West is rather a failure in Russia itself.

Perception of Navalny's activities

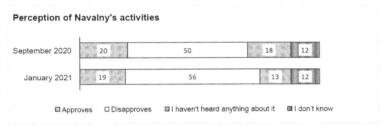

Figure 6 - Perception of Navalny's action. [Source: "The return of Alexei Navalny", Levada Center, February 8, 2021].

The programs *"C dans l'air"* or *"C à vous"* on France 5, which present a relatively objective reality on French domestic affairs, tip over into crude propaganda and often into disinformation when they deal with Russia, China, the Middle East, terrorism and related subjects.

---

249. "The approval of institutions and trust to politician," *Levada Center*, February 26, 2021.
250. www.statista.com/statistics/1099725/russia-constitutional-referendum-participation-intention-by-age/

5. Perceptions and consequences of the case in Russia

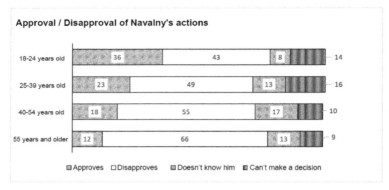

Approval / Disapproval of Navalny's actions

18-24 years old	36	43	8	14
25-39 years old	23	49	13	16
40-54 years old	18	55	17	10
55 years and older	12	66	13	9

▨ Approves ☐ Disapproves ▨ Doesn't know him ■ Can't make a decision

Figure 7 - Approval / disapproval of Navalny's actions by age groups (in %).
[Source: "The return of Alexey Navalny," Levada Center, February 8, 2021].

Among the factors that contribute to discredit Navalny, there is, paradoxically enough, the relative clemency he has enjoyed in Russia. For, as we have seen, contrary to what is said in the West, the authorities have had a relatively light hand with his misdeeds, so as not to give in to Western accusations. To the point that some people in Russia even see it as a sign of collusion between Navalny and the Russian authorities, with the aim of discrediting the opposition... Which is another manifestation of conspiracy.

In February 2021, Navalny appeared in court again: he was sued for defamation by Ignat Sergeevich Artemenko, a 95-year-old World War II veteran, whom he had insulted publicly. The incident seems anecdotal, but has had a disastrous effect on public opinion. For in Russia, veterans of the "Great Patriotic War" are revered as saviors of the nation in the face of Nazism. This case is still ongoing, but it has done much to discredit Navalny in the Russian public opinion[251].

---

251. Mark Episkopos, "What the Navalny Affair Actually Means for Russia," *The National Interest*, February 12, 2021.

The Navalny case

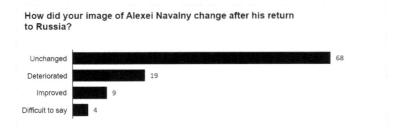

Figure 8 - [Source: "The return of Alexey Navalny", Levada Center, February 8, 2021].

6. Navalny in the service of American politics

In the summer of 2020, under the title "*Pinning Down Putin*" in the magazine *Foreign Affairs*[252], Ambassador Victoria Nuland[253], now Joe Biden's *Under Secretary of State for Political Affairs*, outlined what American policy should be to weaken Russia. Without once mentioning human rights or the rule of law, she defends the principle of intervention in Russian domestic politics and the economy. Although she is a Democrat, she relays the main lines of American foreign policy as practiced by Donald Trump.

It is in this context that Navalny has become - probably in spite of himself - the instrument of the American policy towards Russia; not as a factor of improvement (Navalny has no "program" for his country), but to destabilize Vladimir Putin.

Since the end of the Cold War, the United States has based its security on the dominance of its geostrategic space. They have maintained a distrust of Russia, rooted in the Cold War and fueled by a confusion between Russia and the USSR, which is maintained by certain "experts" on Russia, such as Galia Ackerman or Françoise

---

252. Victoria Nuland, "Pinning Down Putin," *Foreign Affairs*, July/August 2020.
253. Ambassador Victoria Nuland was Deputy Secretary of State for European and Eurasian Affairs during the Ukraine crisis under Barack Obama.

Thom[254]. Contrary to the hopes raised by the "fall of the wall", the United States did not perceive the new international security as the product of cooperation and interdependence in a unified Euro-Atlantic space. They felt legitimized to implement their own foreign policy, for their own benefit, giving Europeans a subsidiary role, as we have seen in Afghanistan, Iraq, Syria, Yemen or the Sahel. This is why, despite the dissolution of the Warsaw Pact, NATO has not fundamentally changed, Russian attempts at rapprochement have all been rejected by the United States, while European attempts to create an autonomous defence have systematically failed.

The U.S., with its aging infrastructure, has the highest number of power outages of any developed country[255] ; explaining them as computer attacks from Russia is a convenient way out[256]. The 2019 Boeing 737 Max flight ban was immediately followed by reports of the situation in the Russian civilian fleet[257].

Repeated military failures in Afghanistan, Iraq, Libya and Syria, the rapid rise of Asia (and China) in technological innovation, and more recently, the poor performance of the United States in managing the Covid crisis have contributed to the image of a country in decline. This explains Donald Trump's *"America First"* policy, taken up by Joe Biden, as evidenced by his March 31, 2021 speech:

> *The rest of the world is closing in [on us] and closing in fast. We can't allow this to continue.*[258]

254. Françoise Thom, "The Russian Party in France," *Commentary*, No. 154, Summer 2016.
255. Ula Chrobak, "The US has more power outages than any other developed country. Here's why," *Popular Science*, August 17, 2020.
256. Sophie Tatum, "US accuses Russia of cyberattacks on power grid," *CNN*, March 18, 2018.
257. Matthew Bodner, "Reports show Russia's terrible aviation record," *Associated Press*, May 7, 2019.
258. "Remarks by President Biden on the American Jobs Plan," Carpenters Pittsburgh Training Center (Pittsburgh, Pennsylvania), *whitehouse.gov*, March 31, 2021.

The aim is to combat countries that could challenge American leadership, first and foremost China (in economic and technological terms) and Russia (in military and geostrategic terms). It is a form of "strategic *mobbing*", whose objective is to isolate them and prevent them from developing constructive relations with other Western countries. This explains, for example, why Antony Blinken, the new American Secretary of State, is threatening his European allies with sanctions if they buy military equipment from Russia[259].

American efforts go far beyond the realm of foreign policy, as it is also about influencing Russia's domestic politics. In February 2021, the *New York Times* summarized the issue very well:

> *"The strategy is this: it is a personalized regime rooted in Putin's popularity," Guriev, the economist close to Navalny, said of the approach. "That is why Putin's popularity must be destroyed."*[260]

To justify this violation of the UN Charter, the promotion of the rule of law or the defense of human rights are invoked. But this is only a pretext, because if the goal appears noble and justified, it is not the objective of the Westerners. A "leaked" memo dated May 17, 2017, addressed to then-Secretary of State Rex Tillerson, sheds light on American and Western duplicity[261] :

> *[... In the case of U.S. allies such as Egypt, Saudi Arabia, and the Philippines, the Administration is absolutely right to*

259. Tal Axelrod, "Blinken warns Turkey, US allies against purchasing Russian weapons," *The Hill*, April 28, 2021.
260. Anton Troianovsky, "A Life in Opposition: Navalny's Path From Gadfly to Heroic Symbol," *The New York Times*, February 13, 2021.
261. www.politico.com/f/?id=00000160-6c37-da3c-a371-ec3f13380001

emphasize good relations for a variety of important reasons, including counterterrorism, and to face honestly the difficult trade-offs in human rights.

[...] With respect to our competitors, the dilemma is less. We do not want to support America's adversaries abroad; we seek to pressure, compete with, and thwart them. For this reason, we should consider human rights as an important issue in U.S. relations with China, Russia, North Korea, and Iran. This is not only because of moral considerations regarding the practices inside these countries. It is also because pressuring these regimes through human rights is a way to impose costs on them, to create counter-pressure and to take back the initiative strategically.

In order to exert pressure on countries such as Russia, China and Iran, the United States has reactivated the tools used to combat the communist threat. In addition to diplomatic action and sanctions, they seek to influence through the channels of the traditional press and by financing organizations in the target countries, whose vocation is clearly subversive.

Like France with *France 24*, *RFI* or *France 5*, or Great Britain with the *BBC*, the United States has press organs dedicated to the war of influence. These are *Radio Free Europe/Radio Liberty* (RFE/RL), *Radio Free Asia* (RFA), *Voice of America* (VOA) and others, placed under the authority of the *Global Media Agency* (USAGM). Their function of influence is such[262] that they are not allowed to communicate on American territory, in order to avoid influencing

---

262. Daniel Lippman, "Deleted Biden video sets off a crisis at Voice of America," *Politico*, July 30, 2020.

elections, as Congressman Brad Sherman noted before the House Foreign Affairs Committee[263].

Their organs of influence are therefore so dangerous for American democracy that they are forbidden to operate on American soil... This sheds light on the ethics of American domestic and foreign policy, supported by our media!

To act through non-governmental actors (NGOs), the United States has the *National Endowment for Democracy* (NED). It was created in 1983 to take over some of the CIA's tasks[264], so that the latter could concentrate on "more muscular" activities. The NED is an NGO (or more precisely: a "quasi-NGO") mainly funded by the US government and Congress. In 1986, the *New York Times* described it as follows:

> *The National Endowment for Democracy, a private group created for this purpose, has channeled a total of $53.7 million in government money to foreign political parties, labor unions, newspapers, magazines, book publishers and other institutions in foreign countries, primarily in countries where democracy is considered fragile or non-existent.*
>
> *Federal money is used for such ventures as aiding the Solidarnosc trade union, printing underground publications in Poland, buying materials for an opposition newspaper in Nicaragua, supporting the opposition in South Korea, helping a party in Northern Ireland that is a member of the Socialist*

263. Committee of *Foreign Affairs*, "Oversight of the United States Agency for Global Media and U.S. International Broadcasting Efforts," *foreignaffairs.house.gov*, September 24, 2020.
264. www.ned.org/about/history/

6. Navalny in the service of American politics

International, and influencing votes in Grenada and Latin American countries. [265]

And I said that the work of the NED *"is similar to the assistance provided by the CIA in the 1950s, 60s and 70s to support pro-American political groups.* Today, its board of directors includes figures such as Elliott Abrams, an ex-diplomat, former clandestine operations in Central America, who organized the illegal financing of the Contras in Nicaragua, cleared those responsible for war crimes in El Salvador[266], perjured himself before Congressional investigative committees and was one of the organizers of the 2002 coup d'état against Hugo Chavez[267].

In particular, the NED supports *Bellingcat*[268], which serves as a front for the CIA's influence operations, as Marc Polymeropoulos, former vice-director of CIA operations in Europe and Eurasia, confessed in *Foreign Policy* magazine: *"I don't want to be too dramatic, but we love it!"*[269] The objective and factual nature of *Bellingcat's* contribution to the Navalny affair is therefore extremely questionable, and casts doubt on the good faith of Westerners.

In reality, NED's support for democracy is very selective: it focuses on countries where the United States seeks to strengthen its influence "behind the scenes. So, for example, it does not fund a program in Saudi Arabia. In Russia, on the other hand, in 2020, the NED maintained no less than 112 influence programs - including

265. David K. Shipler, "Missionaries For Democracy: U.S. Aid For Global Pluralism," *The New York Times*, June 1st 1986.
266. Julian Borger, "US diplomat convicted over Iran-Contra appointed special envoy for Venezuela," *The Guardian*, January 26, 2019.
267. Ed Vulliamy, "Venezuela coup linked to Bush team," *The Guardian*, April 21, 2002.
268. www.bellingcat.com/about/
269. Amy Mackinnon, *"Bellingcat* Can Say What U.S. Intelligence Can't," *Foreign Policy*, December 17, 2020.

support for *"activists"* - for a total amount of 10.6 million dollars![270] Thus, contrary to what Clementine Fauconnier, a "specialist" on Russia, asserts, American interference in Russia is a reality and not simply *"a pillar of the Kremlin's discourse"* to discredit the opposition[271].

On its website, the NED does not specify who receives its funding, but a 2006 cable from the U.S. Embassy in Moscow indicates that it funds Navalny's *Democratic Alternative* movement[272]. A very conservative analysis of the agency's funded projects in 2019-2020 estimates that Navalny and his relatives receive about $1.8 million per year from the United States.

When asked if Navalny is an *"agent of foreigners"*, Galia Ackerman[273], on *France 5*, answers categorically: no. He is not. Let's be clear: Navalny is certainly not a "CIA agent", but the fact that he is financed by foreign countries makes him - technically and legally - a *"foreign agent"* under Russian law. Moreover, the financing of his stay in Germany and of the film by oligarchs based in Israel and London[274], and of his movement by the NED, shows that the United States uses him as a "pawn" in its fight against Russia. In this sense, it can be said that he is a *"foreign agent"*. Moreover, on October 9, 2020, John Brennan, former director of the CIA, tweeted:

---

270. www.ned.org/region/eurasia/russia-2020/
271. Clémentine Fauconnier, in the program "C dans l'air" of February 3, 2020, ("Can Navalny bring down Putin?"), *France 5/YouTube*, February 4, 2021 (25'38")
272. https://wikileaks.org/cable/2006/11/06MOSCOW12709.html; Scott Shane, "Russia Isn't the Only One Meddling in Elections. We Do It, Too," *The New York Times*, February 17, 2018.
273. Galia Ackerman in the program "C dans l'air" of January 28, 2021, ("Poutine / Navalny : espion, poison et corruption #cdanslair 28.01.2021 ", France 5/YouTube, January 29, 2021) (1h01'22").
274. Sabine Siebold, Anton Zverev, Catherine Belton, Andrew Osborn, "Special Report: In Germany's Black Forest, Putin critic Navalny gathered strength and resolve," *Reuters*, 25 February 2021.

6. Navalny in the service of American politics

Imagine the prospects for world peace, prosperity and security if Joe Biden were president of the United States and Alexei Navalny were president of Russia. We are almost halfway there...[275]

Simply put, "We're working on it!"

Beyond foreign policy, the active involvement of Western countries in this affair goes beyond the field of special services, as revealed by the *New York Times*:

Shortly after Navalny's arrival in Berlin, representatives of the Central Intelligence Agency [CIA] and the British Secret Service [MI-6] provided members of the German government with details of the poisoning, including the identities of the Federal Security Service [FSB] agents involved, which directly engaged the Russian government, according to the senior German security official familiar with the case.[276]

So, in less than three days, the Western services already had details on the alleged perpetrators of the poisoning! This information will be used to make the video of December 21, 2020, featuring Alexei Navalny and an "FSB agent."

Let's be clear: there is no indication that this case was created to put pressure on Germany, because, as we have seen, Navalny's poisoning was most likely accidental. On the other hand, the Trump administration most certainly saw the opportunity to exploit it as part of its strategy to isolate Russia and remove its economic resources. Initiated in the summer of 2017, this strategy aims to

---

275. twitter.com/johnbrennan/status/1314587438568833025
276. Michael Schwirtz, "Russian Officers Were Near Navalny When He Was Poisoned, Report Says," *The New York Times*, December 15, 2020.

drive Russia out of its traditional markets[277]. It was complemented, beginning in 2018, by pressure on Germany to abandon the *Nord Stream 2* pipeline[278], followed by sanctions against companies involved in the construction of the pipeline in January 2020[279]. The motion of January 20, 2021, of 58 European parliamentarians (mainly from the former Eastern countries, with a few "Westerners" such as Bernard Guetta), proposing to stop the German-Russian project is in line with the efforts of Donald Trump[280].

No conspiracy here: this strategy was outlined in 2019 by the RAND Corporation[281] *"for the United States and its allies"*, with the objective of *"putting Russia under tension and unbalancing it"*[282]. The idea is to create situations that cause social and economic tensions, which place Russia permanently on the defensive, on several fronts at once, to destabilize and weaken it politically internally and externally.

Its principle is based on the myth - very widespread in France[283] - that the USSR collapsed as a result of an overextension of its capabilities, provoked by Ronald Reagan's "Star Wars" project... The problem is that this is false. As a CIA report of the time already

277. Sarah McFarlane, Georgi Kantchev, "Gas: Trump ready to step on Russian toes in Europe," *L'Opinion*, July 29, 2018.
278. Dpa, "Trump kritisiert Deutschland wegen Ostsee-Pipeline" ("Trump criticizes Germany over Baltic Sea pipeline"), *merkur.de*, 3 April 2018.
279. "Donald Trump approves U.S. sanctions on companies collaborating on Nord Stream 2 pipeline," *Agence Europe*, January 3, 2020.
280. *Joint Motion for a Resolution Pursuant to Rule 132(2) and (4) of the Rules of Procedure on the Arrest of Aleksei Navalny*, European Parliament, 20 January 2021 (2021/2513(RSP)).
281. The RAND Corporation is a think-tank created by the Pentagon at the beginning of the Cold War to develop strategies against the USSR.
282. James Dobbins *et al*, "Overextending and Unbalancing Russia," *RAND Corporation* (Doc. No. RB-10014-A), 2019.
283. Thierry Wolton, *Le KGB en France*, Grasset, 1986.

6. Navalny in the service of American politics

noted, the USSR never engaged in this race[284]. The USSR did not collapse because of Western action, it was the communist system that imploded, because it was not viable. This is why the policy proposed by RAND and implemented by the Biden administration is ill-conceived and counterproductive. Among the measures it proposes in the economic sphere, one recognizes the efforts against the German-Russian gas pipeline, led by Donald Trump until the last days of his mandate[285], and then relayed by some European deputies: to develop energy production in the United States in order to put pressure on Russia's economy, its public spending and, by extension, its defense spending. Incidentally, this would increase world supply and lower world prices, and therefore Russia's income. In addition to being a benefit to the U.S. economy, such a policy does not require multilateral approval;

- impose more severe trade and financial sanctions to degrade the Russian economy;

- push Europe to import gas from suppliers other than Russia, in order to create economic tension in Russia and prevent Europe's dependence on it.

This is a far cry from the European tradition, but the RAND project does not stop there. It discerns the subversion of the Russian political system, where both the measures taken to support Navalny and the NED-funded projects are recognized (see Table 7).

---

284. "Moscow's Response to US Plans for Missile Defense," *Internet archive* (web.archive.org/web/20170119110741/https://www.cia.gov/library/readingroom/docs/DOC_0006122438.pdf).
285. Faustine Vincent, Nabil Wakim, "Les États-Unis accentuent les sanctions contre le gazoduc Nord Stream 2," *Le Monde*, January 5, 2021.

Options for imposing costs on Russia

High cost ideological and informational options	Probability of success in Russia's capacity overextension	Benefits (for the United States)	Costs and risks (for Russia)
Decreasing confidence in the Russian electoral system	low	means	high
Create the perception that the plan is not in the public interest	average	means	high
Encourage internal protests and other non-violent resistance	low	means	high
Undermining Russia's image abroad	average	means	means

Table 7 - Options for imposing costs on Russia in the areas of politics and information. One recognizes the axes of the media campaign that accompanied the Navalny case in the West. [Source: "Overextending and Unbalancing Russia," RAND Corporation, 2019 (p. 5).

What is striking about this document, which contains some 30 major recommendations, is that at *no point* does it mention the promotion of human rights or the rule of law. This confirms an observation made earlier: the Navalny case is used as a lever to support a policy that has nothing to do with improving the situation in Russia, but only serves the interests of the United States[286].

Unlike the USSR, where only 5 to 9% of the population was communist, today 60 to 65% of Russians approve of Vladimir Putin's

286. "Trump schaltet sich im Fall Nawalny ein und kritisiert Nord Stream 2" ("Trump intervenes in the Navalny case and criticizes Nord Stream 2"), *Handelsblatt*, September 5, 2020; "Trump fordert Stopp von Nord Stream 2" ("Trump calls for a stop to Nord Stream 2"), *Der Spiegel*, September 7, 2020.

6. Navalny in the service of American politics

actions. Thus, during the Cold War, with a population that suffered from the regime, pro-Western propaganda was enough to hope to destabilize the USSR. Today, the situation is very different: however imperfect it may be, the Russian government is not out of step with its population. Propaganda is no longer enough to destabilize: it is necessary to disinform. This is why the West has had to set up structures for this purpose.

The Navalny affair is part of this framework, in which allied initiatives complement the American mechanism. These include the NATO *Strategic Communication Center of Excellence* (STRATCOM)[287] and the British *Integrity Initiative* (II). Created in the aftermath of the Ukrainian crisis, the latter was only revealed to the public at the end of 2018 by an *Anonymous* hack[288]. At that point, Russian intelligence services were naturally accused of running a disinformation campaign against NATO. This is not impossible, but there is no evidence of it at this stage, as the documents revealed - including lists of names of NI agents and correspondents abroad - appear to be authentic. In November 2018, the British government actually confirmed that it was funding this initiative[289].

The II was created under the aegis of the British Foreign Office (FCO), which is responsible for the *Secret Intelligence Service* (MI-6) and the *Government Communications Headquarters* (GCHQ) in charge of cyber warfare, which are associated with this initiative. It is funded by the British Ministry of Defence and the army, the Lithuanian Ministry of Defence and NATO, and aims to combat Russian disinformation in Europe. It uses the *BBC* and *Reuters* to

---

287. www.stratcomcoe.org/
288. telegra.ph/OP-HMG-Trojan-Horse-Part-4-Undermining-Russia-I-02-04
289. *Foreign and Commonwealth Office: Integrity Initiative, Question for Foreign and Commonwealth Office*, UIN 196177, November 27, 2018.

promote an "official" narrative. It includes computer marketing networks and private intelligence agencies such as *Bellingcat,* and relies on national "clusters" composed of correspondents in each participating country. It questions.

First, in its context. The mere creation of a governmental authority to "manage" information, with ramifications in some countries, takes us far away from the principles of democracy to combat disinformation. During seventy years of the Cold War, Western propaganda was countered by Soviet disinformation, with a subversive effect on both sides of the "Iron Curtain. Yet Western strategy remained "Darwinian," based on the principle that "good" information naturally drives out "bad. Apart from a few attempts to control it, such as the CIA's Operation MOCKINGBIRD[290], Western countries did not feel the need to set up structures to "correct" information, because the diversity of information guaranteed its quality. Are we therefore obliged, today, to have structures that determine what is the "good information" that must drive out the "bad"?

Second, in terms of its resources. The most disturbing aspect of the British initiative is that the members of the national "clusters" belong to official or reputedly independent institutions. For example, in France, British officials made the first contacts with government officials in early 2016. After a meeting in Paris in May, they note:

> *The French are very nationalistic, anti-American. There is also admiration for brute force ("the Napoleon complex"). As a result, there is a clear tendency to admire Putin, combined*

---

290. Lauren Von Bernuth, "Operation Mockingbird - The CIA's History of Media Manipulation," *medium.com*, April 10, 2018.

6. Navalny in the service of American politics

with a historical feeling of closeness to Russia that makes them
sympathize with Russia.[291]

The result will be the creation, *"independently of the government"*,
of the *"Integrity France"* cluster. To what extent the lists of names
revealed in 2018 are complete and still correct is uncertain, but
they question the integrity of the institutions that inform or brief
our politicians. They include journalists, officials from the Ministry
of Foreign Affairs, the *General Secretariat of Defense and National
Security* (SGDSN), Rudy Reichstadt of *Conspiracy Watch*[292],
Françoise Thom (a fierce opponent of foreign paid media (!) and
diplomatic dialogue with Russia[293]) or Galia Ackerman, who regularly speaks on *France 5* about Russia. In the Belgian cluster (2019),
there are NATO and European Union officials, as well as researchers
from the *Université libre de Bruxelles*; in the Swiss cluster (2019),
there are people paid by the Swiss Ministry of Defense. In the British
cluster, unsurprisingly, there is *Bellingcat* and Vladimir Achourkov,
a close collaborator of Navalny.

Technically, individuals who are employed by one government
but at the same time work underhandedly for the benefit of another
in an influencing activity fit the definition of *"agents of influence"*[294].
This is a situation where employees of national governments may
have conflicts of interest with the policy decisions of their employer.

291. CND Paris & Brussels 2-4 May 2016 (https://www.pdf-archive.com/2018/12/13/
cnd-paris--bxl-may-2016-v2/).
292. Benoît Bréville, "Chasseur de "conspis"", *Le Monde diplomatique*, April-May 2018;
Brice Perrier, "Conspiracy Watch de Rudy Reichstadt : les contradictions de l'anti-com-
plotiste professionnel", *Marianne*, November 23, 2019; Laurent Dauré, "Quand les 'com-
plotologues' de Franceinfo font l'impasse sur la principale théorie du complot de l'ère
Trump", *Acrimed*, March 10, 2021.
293. Isabelle Mandraud, "Françoise Thom, la procureur de Poutine," *Le Monde*, October 21, 2019.
294. en.wikipedia.org/wiki/Influencer

This contributes to what some call the "deep state," which can generate dynamics different from those intended by the elected authorities. This can lead to situations comparable to that of France towards Germany, when Clément Beaune, Secretary of State for European Affairs, publicly spoke out in favour of abandoning the *Nord Stream 2* project[295] because of the Navalny affair, forcing Yves Le Drian, and then Emmanuel Macron, to clarify that France considers the two cases to be separate[296].

Third, as to the purpose of the II. The examples presented in its "*guide*" show that it is directed against Russia's responses to Western accusations (the Skripal affair, the MH-17 disaster in Ukraine, the annexation of Crimea, cyber-attacks...), which have never been demonstrated or remain unexplained[297]. As described, the role of NI is essentially to discredit Russia's responses to the attacks it is subjected to. This is in line with the strategy developed by the RAND Corporation seen above. In June 2018, during a meeting organized by the FCO to mobilize support for influence operations, the objective of the operation is clearly stated: "*The program aims to weaken Russia's influence over its neighbors*"[298], without mentioning once the rule of law or human rights. It is therefore not a question of improving our relations with Russia or consolidating the rule of law there, but only of weakening it.

---

295. "Affaire Navalny: la France favorable à l'abandon du projet de gazoduc Nord Stream 2, selon le secrétaire d'État chargé des Affaires européennes", *franceinfo.fr*, February 1st 2021.
296. "France will not intervene with Germany on Nord Stream 2, says Le Drian," *Reuters*, February 3, 2021.
297. The Integrity Initiative Guide to Countering Russian Disinformation (https://www.pdf-archive.com/2018/11/02/untitled-pdf-document-1/)
298. *Supplier Event, Support for Independent Media in Eastern Partnership Countries, Support for Independent Media in the Baltic States*, Foreign & Commonwealth Office, London, 26 June 2018.

6. Navalny in the service of American politics

The United States sees the convergence of two threats in energy: Europe's dependence on Russia and competition for its own production. This is why the Americans are opposed to the *Nord Stream 2* gas pipeline project, linking Russia to Germany. It is in this context that the Navalny affair comes at the right time.

Finally and fundamentally, it is the principle of objective and independent information, guarantor of the rule of law, that is at stake here. The problem is not so much the response to the information coming from Russia, as the spirit and ethics we put into it. Moreover, the II is a tool whose use can drift quite quickly, for example when it is a question of leading a campaign against the Labour Party in Great Britain[299].

---

299. Chris York, "How A Murky Row Over Russia, Jeremy Corbyn And A 'Psyops Campaign' Went Mainstream," *huffingtonpost.co.uk*, February 2, 2019; Mark McLaughlin, "Hacker-hit research group the Integrity Initiative is sorry for Jeremy Corbyn tweets," *The Times*, April 6, 2019.

7. Conclusions

7.1. The Navalny case

The analysis of the Navalny case shows that at each of its stages, in the spectrum of possible explanations, those were systematically chosen that fit into the narrative of a poisoning with Novitchok, therefore ordered by Vladimir Putin. The fact that the symptoms of Skripal and Navalny were totally different, that neither of them had *the symptoms of* nerve agent poisoning, that neither of them had the long-term after-effects associated with Novitchok poisoning, or that Novitchok was also produced by Western countries, did not prompt either the media or politicians to be cautious.

On the contrary, on the sole basis of the so-called telephone confession of an agent, whose identity and quality no one has been able to verify, and of military reports that have remained secret, a foreign policy is being shaped and measures are being taken with uncertain consequences.

The reports of the German, French, Swedish and OPCW laboratories are classified, so we do not know their content. However, it is reasonable to assume that if their findings had clearly identified the presence of Novitchok, they would have been published in greater detail. In this situation, under the threat of U.S. sanctions in the context of the *Nord Stream 2* project, Germany could hardly officially publish results contrary to the U.S. narrative. It probably sought to exploit the change of administration in Washington to extricate itself from it, both by driving a wedge into the Trump administration's narrative and by offering Europe the opportunity for a dignified exit from the crisis. So she allowed German doctors to publish their analyses, which tend to indicate poisoning due to a bad combination of alcohol and drugs, and thus contradict the accusations against Russia.

We note that neither the European parliamentarians nor the UN experts took into account the analyses published by German doctors, and at no time did they seek to exploit the opportunities opened up by the different diagnoses of civilians and soldiers. On the contrary, they deliberately dismissed anything that might have discredited the Western accusations. As Bernard Guetta perfectly illustrates, the problem of our politicians and governments is their inability to distinguish between "suspicions" and "certainties", which feeds a dogmatic foreign policy far from the interest of Europeans and damages their credibility.

Assuming that Navalny was intentionally poisoned by the Russian government, it is reasonable to ask whether the political threat he poses is commensurate with the political risk of his removal. One would have to be naive, like Bernard Guetta, or see a lot of movies, to think that a government would take such a risk for such a paltry threat. However, unlike leaders like Donald Trump or Emmanuel Macron, Vladimir Putin has always been extremely rational in his choices.

We are in a situation where the political risk of failure is greater than the gain from success. A problem that, for example, would only marginally affect a criminal network. On the BBC, Mark Galeotti, Russia expert at the *Royal United Services Institute* (RUSI) said:

> *The Russian state seems to have been caught off guard, which implies that this was not a centrally planned operation.... This suggests that it was the act of a powerful Russian, but not necessarily of the state.*[300]

Moreover, *Euronews*, *Tribune de Genève* and *Le Point* report that Navalny has *"hundreds of enemies, including determined individuals"*[301] because of his fight against corruption. Moreover, the numerous lawsuits against Navalny - of which we have cited a few examples - do not come from the government, but from oligarchs and private figures. It is therefore not unreasonable to think that other actors affected by his investigations into corruption - especially in organized crime circles - might have an *existential* interest in suppressing him.

This is why Vladimir Putin cynically states: *"If we had wanted to, the case would have been carried out!"*[302] Obviously, if there had been a real desire to eliminate Navalny, they would probably have used a method that does not remind of the Skripal affair and that is more effective (!), without pointing the finger at Russia.

---

300. Laurence Peter, "Navalny and Russia's arsenal of exotic poisons," *BBC News*, August 26, 2020.
301. "No poison in Navalny's body," *Tribune de Genève*, August 21, 2020; Joanne Massard with AFP, "His health condition deemed 'unstable', Alexei Navalny will not be able to be transferred abroad," *euronews.com*, August 21, 2020; AFP, "Navalny: a plane on its way to pick up the Russian opponent in serious condition," *Le Point*, August 21, 2020.
302. AFP, "For Vladimir Putin, if Russia had wanted to poison Navalny, he would be dead," *Le Figaro*, December 17, 2020.

7. Conclusions

However, the "services" have poisons that are virtually undetectable at autopsy...[303]

In spite of this, although no concrete verifiable facts confirm it, the idea that it is the work of the Russian secret services prevails. Thus, from the beginning of September 2020, even before the French, Swedish and OPCW laboratories had begun their analyses, *Conspiracy Watch "knows"* that he was poisoned with Novitchok, *"rather associated with the Russian secret services"*, and qualifies as *"conspiracy"* the possibility that the poisoning could be the work of organized crime[304]. This way of excluding all alternative explanations, of asserting a judgment based on information that is all speculative, of ignoring certain facts and linking others with arbitrary logic corresponds exactly to the definition of conspiracy[305]. The "anti-conspiracy people" become... "conspiracy people"!

7.2. The impact on international relations

The Navalny affair occurs in a context where diplomatic action has traded cooperation for sanction. Influenced by the United States, magnified under the presidency of Donald Trump and prolonged by Joe Biden, this way of managing international relations departs from the European tradition of diplomacy by replacing dialogue with a trial of strength. For Europe is the willing victim of this degradation, both ethical and political: the media and politicians who

---

303. Viktor Popenko, Секретные Инструкции ЦРУ и КГБ по Сбору Фактов, Конспирации и Дезинформации ("Secret Instructions of the CIA and KGB on Fact-Finding, Conspiracy and Disinformation") AST, Moscow, 2014, p. 258.
304. Antoine Hasday, *op. cit.*
305. en.wikipedia.org/wiki/Complot_Theory

accused Donald Trump of lies have slavishly accepted and relayed his accusations against Russia, China, Iran and others.

To what extent is the Russian political system democratic is an open question. To answer this question, one must also understand that, seen from Switzerland, France is nothing more than an elective monarchy, where democracy is reduced to its most basic expression: decisions are erratic, the popular vote - when it exists - is flouted, freedom of the press and freedom of opinion are far from total, and politicians are secretly monitored[306] ; in 2018-2019, during the Yellow Vests crisis more than 40,000 people were convicted of various offenses and misdemeanors *"on the basis of vague laws [...] used to illegally restrict the rights to freedom of peaceful assembly and freedom of expression"*[307].

Ultimately, the issue is not who is for or against Russia, or whether or not it respects the rule of law. It is not even a question of whether U.S. hegemony is good or bad, and whether it cheats or not to achieve its goals. The real question is whether our way of leading it to democracy is relevant. In April 2021, Emmanuel Macron had an approval rating of 37%[308], while Vladimir Putin's was 65%, after the pro-Navalny protests[309]. Under these circumstances, what gives us the right to impose a "regime" change in Russia from outside and not in France?

In February 2021, the arrest of Pablo Hasél in Spain for his separatist views, and the demonstrations that followed, did not trigger European sanctions. The detention of Julian Assange in

---

306. T.B., J.M.Dé., "Une curieuse enquête secrète sur Nicolas Sarkozy", *leparisien.fr*, 24 June 2020 (updated 25 June 2020).

307. "France/right to protest. Amnesty International denounces the arrests and prosecutions of thousands of peaceful protesters in France before and during the Covid-19 pandemic," *amnesty.co.uk*, 29 September 2020.

308. "The Political Observatory - March 2021," *elabe.fr*, March 4, 2021.

309. www.levada.ru/en/

7. Conclusions

Great Britain, for having disclosed American war crimes, curiously enough does not arouse the passion of our media - messages of support are even deleted by Twitter![310] Our democracies talk about the rule of law, but accept that Sweden fabricates a rape accusation against Assange[311]. Fingers are immediately pointed at Russia and sanctions are applied on the basis of very vague elements and rumors in the Navalny case, but the murder of Jamal Khashoggi is put into perspective. Daniel Hale, a former US Air Force officer and whistleblower on illegal drone actions by the US, is arrested and jailed before he has even been tried on charges deemed vague by his lawyers[312]. Facebook deletes accounts favorable to Qassem Soleimani after his assassination[313]. Pro-Russia views are labeled as "conspiratorial" or "*Russia-related*," even though we don't know; and Twitter closes accounts that could "*undermine faith in NATO*"[314] ! Even during the Cold War, such arguments were never used!

The Navalny affair is both an opportunity for the United States to discredit Vladimir Putin and a distraction for European countries from their own domestic problems. The images of the January 2021 demonstrations in Moscow are repeated on our screens: they mask the demonstrations against the law on global security or the opponents of the Covid measures, as well as the questionable European management of vaccines...

---

310. Mike Head, "Twitter removes account of Assange defense organization," *wsws.org*, July 13, 2019.
311. Daniel Ryser, Yves Bachmann, Charles Hawley, *op. cit.*
312. Alex Emmons, "Drone Whistleblower Daniel Hale Jailed Ahead of Sentencing," *The Intercept*, May 6, 2021.
313. Zena Chamas, "Facebook admits censoring posts supporting slain Iranian General Qassem Soleimani," *abc.net*, January 14, 2020.
314. "Disclosing networks of state-linked information operations," *Twitter Safety*, February 23, 2021.

Promoting democracy and human rights in the world is a noble and necessary task. But only if we do it in a sincere and honest way (which is far from being the case), and in a less childish way.

The constant hammering against Russia tends to stimulate Russian national pride and become counterproductive. It generates more support for the Putin government, which turns against Navalny himself. The "debunking" of his film has exposed a costly deception, obviously carried out with external financial assistance; the disproportionate support of the West for his movement, the all too visible assistance of the American and British secret services, revealed by the *New York Times*, is pushing the Russian population to question Navalny himself and his role in a climate of sanctions and ruptures.

In January 2021, Nikolai Patrushev, Secretary of the Security Council of the Russian Federation and former head of the FSB, claimed that Alexei Navalny was being used by Western countries to destabilize the Russian domestic situation[315]. It is known that the Russian population is sensitive to this argument, which contributes to Navalny's unpopularity. In February 2021, the FSB released a video showing Navalny's collaborator Vladimir Ashurkov discussing $10-20 million in financial aid with British diplomat James Ford (identified as a British MI-6 agent) in 2012[316]. In fact, this video (whose authenticity has not been questioned) does not demonstrate much, as Ford does not grant anything and asks Ashurkov to apply to the NGO *Transparency International*, but it does reinforce Russian opinion.

315. "West using Navalny to destabilize Russia by creating social upheaval & encouraging unrest, says Russian security chief Patrushev," *RT*, January 26, 2021.
316. Video "Top Navalny aide asked alleged British spy for millions in funding - FSB intelligence video claims," *RT*, February 1st 2021, *YouTube* (youtube.com/watch?v=k227KvK-FYN8).

7. Conclusions

Therefore, it is surprising that Western institutions and politicians are loudly supporting Navalny and using sanctions to demand his release. As the *Levada Center*'s investigations show, they only strengthen support for the government. This confirms the fact that our politicians do not seek to promote the rule of law or human rights, but to weaken Russia.

This is how Western sanctions seek to create an untenable situation for local populations, so that they rebel against their government. This is the same principle that is applied to Iran, Syria, Cuba, Venezuela, etc. It is a variant of the doctrine that justified the bombing of civilian populations in Germany as early as 1943, in Serbia in 1990, in Iraq in 2003, in Lebanon in 2006, in Gaza in 2014: it is a matter of inciting populations to revolt against their authorities, in order to promote regime change. This principle is clearly described by Richard Nephew, head of sanctions at the State Department under Obama and delegate to Iran under Joe Biden, in a book entitled *The Art of Sanctions, the* spirit of which can clearly be described as repugnant[317]. Thus, on *France 5*, Bernard Guetta declares that "*the standard of living is constantly falling in Russia partly, but only partly, because of sanctions or thanks to Western sanctions [...]*[318] "... How weak are the values of someone who is proud to lower the living conditions of a people!

This is a way of holding people hostage, leading "color revolutions" and imposing an alternative leadership that is far from representing their people and their grievances. So it is with Juan Guaidó in Venezuela, who is financing a coup attempt with

---

317. Richard Nephew, *The Art of Sanctions - A View from the Field*, Columbia University Press, New York, 2018.
318. Bernard Guetta, in " Le 5 sur 5 ! - C à Vous - 03/02/2021 ", *France 5/YouTube*, February 3, 2021 (17'10")

American mercenaries[319], who is unable to mobilize the population to take power[320], and who was finally abandoned by his own party, to the point that the European Union had to give up considering him as *"interim president"*[321]... But he remains the only president of Venezuela recognized by Emmanuel Macron...[322]

When Donald Trump claims that he was the victim of fraud and that he won the election against Joe Biden we realize - with good reason - that he is lying; even though the American electoral system means that it all came down to a mere 22,091 votes, or 0.01%, the narrowest margin in American history[323]. But when Belarusian opponent Svetlana Tikhanovskaya claims to have won the election in August 2020[324], she is believed without question, or really knowing her. However, with 9.9% of the vote, the opposition's result is consistent with previous elections. This does not mean that there was no fraud at the local level, but most likely not such as to alter the overall outcome of the election to the point of triggering international sanctions[325]. Moreover, this was the first time in twenty-nine years that the OSCE had not sent observers to the

---

319. "Read the attachments to the General Services Agreement between the Venezuelan opposition and Silvercorp," *The Washington Post*, May 7, 2020.
320. Joshua Goodman, Christopher Torchia, "How the Venezuelan 'coup' didn't get beyond street demonstrations supporting Juan Guaido," *Associated Press/USA Today*, May 1st 2019.
321. "EU states no longer recognize Guaido as Venezuela's interim president," *Reuters*, January 25, 2021.
322. Status as of the end of February 2021.
323. James M. Lindsay, "The 2020 Election by the Numbers," *The Council of Foreign Relations*, December 15, 2020.
324. Emmanuel Grynszpan, "Svetlana Tikhanovskaya, du triomphe à l'exil en vingt-quatre heures", *letemps.ch*, August 11, 2020 (updated August 12, 2020).
325. "Belarus: EU imposes sanctions for repression and falsification of election results," *Council of the European Union*, October 2, 2020.

7. Conclusions

elections[326], despite Belarus' request[327]. To legitimize support for Svetlana Tikhanovskaya, it was claimed that one of the main causes of discontent in Belarus was the *"disastrous management of the pandemic"*[328], even though the figures clearly show the opposite (see Figure 9).

Comparison of Covid mortality between France, Russia and Belarus

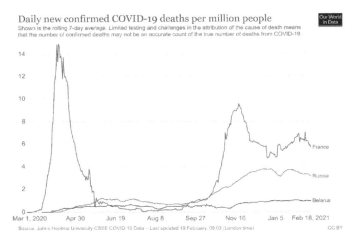

Figure 9 - As can be seen, the allegation of Covid mismanagement in Belarus is misinformation.

---

326. "ODIHR will not deploy election observation mission to Belarus due to lack of invitation," *OSCE Office for Democratic Institutions and Human Rights,* July 15, 2020.
327. "Given that the OSCE Copenhagen Document provides for a standing invitation to observe, a formal invitation to observe elections is in principle not necessary. However, the practice has been for participating States to issue a written invitation to the ODIHR in a timely manner to reaffirm their commitments and willingness to receive international observers," *Election Observation Handbook: Sixth Edition, OSCE,* June 11, 2010, paragraph 4.1.
328. "En Biélorussie, trois femmes défient "le dernier dictateur d'Europe"', *rts.ch,* 10 August 2020; Jean-Yves Camus, "Biélorussie : ni Moscou ni Bruxelles", *charliehebdo.fr,* 19 August 2020; "L'avenir de l'Europe se joue aussi à Minsk", *Ouest-France,* 6 February 2021.

The explanation for these paradoxes is that in reality we do not support these opponents *for* their value, but *against* their governments. Thus, Bernard Guetta, European deputy of *La République en marche,* takes up the cause of Navalny, a far-right nationalist activist[329], who approves the annexation of Crimea[330] (and declares in *The Moscow Times*[331] that he would not give it back if he were in power[332]), who has never expressed a concrete project for Russia, who has sought to enrich himself through embezzlement, and who does not represent any of the values that Europe claims to defend! As Emma Ashford and Mathew Burrows of the *Atlantic Council* - though associated with NATO - noted in March 2021[333] : we are not in a fight *for* democracy and the rule of law, but *against* the influence of Russia. We are technically conducting a counter-productive policy of subversion (the phenomenon of asymmetry): it only reinforces the importance of Asia at the expense of Europe, without reinforcing any of our values.

329. Gaël de Santis, "Navalny: a Russian nationalist," *L'Humanité*, March 27, 2017.
330. "What Does Aleksey Navalny Really Think About Ukraine, Crimea And Donbas?", *ukraineworld.org*, 21 January 2021.
331. Alec Luhn, "Hackers target Russian newspaper site accused of being anti-Putin," *The Guardian*, February 5, 2015.
332. Anna Dolgov, "Navalny Wouldn't Return Crimea, Considers Immigration Bigger Issue Than Ukraine," *The Moscow Times*, October 16, 2014.
333. Emma Ashford, Mathew Burrows, "Reality Check #4: Focus on interests, not on human rights with Russia," *atlanticcouncil.org*, 5 March 2021.

7. Conclusions

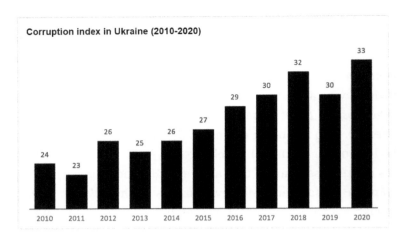

Corruption index in Ukraine (2010-2020)

Figure 10 - Contrary to claims, the Mayan Revolution in 2014 was not about fighting corruption, but about reducing Russia's sphere of influence in Eastern Europe. [Source: tradingeconomics.com/ukraine/corruption-index]

For example, in 2014, it was claimed that *"regime corruption is the main cause of protests in Ukraine"*[334]. Yet, despite (or perhaps, because of) its rapprochement with NATO and the European Union, corruption has grown significantly (see Figure 10). This has led the *International Monetary Fund* (IMF) to deny Ukraine aid in 2021[335].

In reality, it was more about cutting ties with Russia than fighting corruption. Instead of seeing the Ukrainian crisis as an opportunity, it was seen as an act of war. In the *Washington Post*, Henry Kissinger, Ronald Reagan's national security adviser, noted that the European Union *"helped turn a negotiation into a crisis"* and rightly observed:

---

334. Clément Chenaux, "Ukraine: 'Corruption is everywhere, it's the main cause of the revolt,' " *lexpress.fr*, February 22, 2014 (updated February 24, 2014).
335. AFP, "Ukraine : pas d'aide du FMI, davantage de réformes exigées", *lefigaro.fr*, 13 February 2021 (updated 14 February 2021).

[...] the demonization of Vladimir Putin is not a policy; it is an
alibi for not having one.[336]

The proof that we do not seek to promote our values, but to "crush" those who do not have the same ones, is the fact that the United States does not hesitate to impose sanctions on its European allies when their foreign policy deviates from its own. In particular when they concern Iran or Cuba. This is the case with the Covid-19 crisis. Thus, the 2020 edition of the annual report of the U.S. *Department of Health and Human Services* (HHS), proudly describes its record:

> *Combating Harmful Influences in the Americas: The Office of Global Affairs [OGA] has used diplomatic relations in the Americas region to weaken states, including Cuba, Venezuela, and Russia, that are working to increase their influence in the region at the expense of U.S. safety and security. OGA has coordinated with other U.S. government agencies to strengthen diplomatic relations and offer technical and humanitarian assistance to dissuade countries in the region from accepting aid from these rogue states. Examples include using the OGA health attaché's office to persuade Brazil to reject Russia's Covid-19 vaccine, and offering CDC technical assistance to Panama instead of Cuban doctors.*[337]

We use our "values" as a means of pressure on others, but we ourselves have totally abandoned them, along with our ethics, in the management of international relations. We practice exactly what the Russian government is accused of...

---

336. Henry A. Kissinger, "How the Ukraine Crisis Ends," *The Washington Post*, March 5, 2014.
337. *Annual Report 2020*, US Department of Health and Human Services, Washington DC, January 2021.

We do not fight tyranny by justifying other tyrannies, and we do not fight abuse by tolerating only our own. Our conception of international relations increasingly defies political ethics and the law. Have the United States and Britain been condemned for lying to the UN Security Council before the war in Iraq? Have those who deliberately lied to public opinion to justify the intervention in Libya been condemned? Has anyone condemned the bombing of civilian populations with the sole aim of inciting them to turn against their leaders in the former Yugoslavia, Iraq, Syria or Libya? Do we adopt sanctions against Israel which applies its doctrine of "*disproportionate use of force*" (Dahiya Doctrine) against civilians? Obviously not. We accept that dishonest generals, ignorant diplomats, lying philosophers or corrupt presidents distort reality to abuse democratic institutions and the mandate given to them by the voters. Our political elites support individuals with dubious values, who are far from unanimous in their country.

In the Skripal and Navalny cases, Britain and Germany have demanded clarification from Russia, but neither has provided Russia with the "incriminating" evidence in their possession, as required by the *European Convention on Mutual Assistance*[338] and the *Chemical Weapons Convention*[339]. Because in fact we are not in a position to prove our accusations and confront Russia with them. Because we are not looking for justice or respect for the law, but simply to weaken Russia's credibility and influence. The same pattern is applied to China. That is why journalists and parliamen-

---

338. *European Convention on Mutual Assistance in Criminal Matters*, Council of Europe, 20 April 1959 (Article 1).
339. *Convention on the Prohibition of the Development, Production, Stockpiling and Use of Chemical Weapons and on their Destruction* (Article IX - Consultation, Cooperation and Fact-Finding) (with amendments through June 7, 2020), www.opcw.org (opcw.org/fileadmin/OPCW/CWC/CWC_en.pdf).

tarians who are so vehement against Russia and China are so silent and complacent - even complicit - about human rights violations by US allies.

Beyond an imagery stemming from the Cold War and carried by politicians and journalists who did not really know it, the origin of this war of influence is probably internal to Western countries. In the United States, the Russian threat became an argument between Democrats and Republicans: the aim was to discredit Donald Trump and facilitate his impeachment by accusing Russia of having made him get elected, under the pretext that Putin was "holding him" with compromising documents. Thus, the daily *Le Temps* claimed that Trump was *under* Putin's *influence*[340], *Le Point* claimed that there was collusion between them[341], *Le Journal de Montréal* declared that "*Putin adores Trump*"[342], *Le Monde* claimed that "*Putin believes in Trump*"[343] and *Radio-Canada* that Putin would have sought to have Trump re-elected in 2020[344]. Indeed, *Le Figaro* saw a "*positive alchemy*" between the two men[345], to the point that, according to *La Croix*, Trump preferred Putin to his NATO partners[346]. We are in the middle of political fiction. But that's not all: the day after the Capitol Hill riot, on January 19, 2021, Hillary Clinton tweeted to Nancy Pelosi that Trump had received orders from Putin:

340. Stéphane Bussard, "Trump, un "candidat mandchou"?", *letemps.ch*, September 28, 2020 (updated September 29, 2020).

341. AFP, "Donald Trump: why his links with Russia question," *lepoint.fr*, January 14, 2019 (updated January 15, 2019).

342. Loïc Tassé, "Why Putin loves Trump", *Le Journal de Montréal*, February 22, 2020.

343. Benoît Vitkine, ""*In Trump we still trust*": the American campaign as seen from Russia," *Le Monde*, October 27, 2020.

344. "Putin 'likely' leading operation to help Trump's re-election," *ici.radio-canada.ca*, September 22, 2020.

345. Nicolas Barotte, "Trump-Putin: face-to-face on a background of crises," *Le Figaro*, July 7, 2017.

346. François d'Alançon, "Nato caught between Trump and Putin," *La Croix*, July 11, 2018.

7. Conclusions

I don't think we know who they all are yet. I hope history will
tell us who he is beholden to, who is pulling the strings [...]. I'd
like to see his phone records to see if he had talked to Putin the
day the insurgents invaded our Capitol. [347]

Putin even becomes a weapon within the Democratic Party: the Democrats Bernie Sanders[348] and the excellent Tulsi Gabbard[349] are alternately accused of being *"preferred by the Russians"* or even of being *"Russian spies"* by their own party, in order to clear the way for Joe Biden!

It is also clear that the Navalny affair has put Germany in a diplomatic bind with both the Americans and the Russians. But not only do our politicians sacrifice their values to their prejudices, they also abandon European solidarity to support American policy!

In Europe, the problem is more complex. It is often forgotten that the Baltic States and the Ukraine were briefly "liberated" from the Soviets by the Nazis, and that the armed struggle against the USSR was led, until the 1960s, by clandestine networks supported by NATO[350], created from the networks set up with ex-Waffen-SS

347. twitter.com/i/status/1351297926769872899
348. George Zornick, "Bernie Sanders Is a Russian Agent, and Other Things I Learned This Week," *The Nation*, June 16, 2017; "Bernie Sanders Briefed by U.S. Officials that Russia is Trying to Help His Presidential Campaign," *The Washington Post*, February 21, 2020; Sydney Ember, "Russia Is Said to Be Interfering to Aid Sanders in Democratic Primaries," *The New York Times*, February 26, 2020.
349. Dan Merica, "Hillary Clinton suggests Russians are 'grooming' Tulsi Gabbard for third-party run," *CNN*, October 21, 2019; Natalie Tabibian, "Could Tulsi Gabbard be a Russian Spy?", *milkenroar.com*, November 12, 2019; Tim Marcin, "Here's Exactly How Much Russian Media Loves Tulsi Gabbard - and Hates Biden," *Vice News*, November 19, 2019.
350. Cristina Maza, "Veterans of World War II-Era Nazi SS Special Forces March in Latvia As Europe Experiences Wave of Far-Right Nationalism," *Newsweek*, March 19, 2018; Cnaan Liphshiz, "Jewish community protests after plaque honoring SS officer unveiled in Estonia," *The Times of Israel*, June 30, 2018; Paul Kirby, "Lithuania monument for 'Nazi collaborator' prompts diplomatic row," *BBC News*, May 8, 2019.

in 1944. Thus, the 2nd SS division "Das Reich", responsible for the massacre of Oradour-sur-Glane in France, is admired in Ukraine where it "liberated" Kharkov[351]. This explains why in the Baltic countries - the most virulent against Russia - de-Sovietization was carried out to the detriment of the Russian-speaking fraction of their population. In Latvia and Estonia, where Russian speakers make up 20 to 25 per cent of the population, they have the status of "*non-citizens*" (in Lithuania, they enjoy a more liberal status and have access to Lithuanian nationality). The hatred of Russia, largely fanned by the West, has gone so far that Ukraine has refused to approve the Russian vaccine Sputnik V[352] and is reduced to "*hoping*" to receive it from another country![353] Treating their Russian-speaking minorities badly with our blessing, these countries fear that Russia will invoke the "*responsibility to protect*" (R2P), defined by the United Nations, to intervene[354].

In fact, we are solving nothing and erecting additional barriers, often unjustified and sterile. Our leaders are caught in the middle of a multitude of complex and often contradictory problems: nuclear energy versus carbon emissions; humanitarian temptation and immigration problems; religious freedom and security; productivity and jobs; national sovereignty and the European ideal; the fight against terrorism and international law; the fight against coronavirus and the economy, etc. In Afghanistan, Iraq, Libya, Syria or Mali, our aimless wars have become endless failures. The Covid crisis is the most recent and striking example of measures taken

---

351. Alec Luhn, "Preparing for War With Ukraine's Fascist Defenders of Freedom," *Foreign Policy*, August 30, 2014.

352. "Ukraine formally bans registration of Russian COVID-19 vaccines," *Reuters*, February 10, 2021.

353. Natalia Zinets, "Ukraine hopes to get some COVID-19 vaccines from other states," *Reuters*, February 8, 2021.

354. www.un.org/en/genocideprevention/about-responsibility-to-protect.shtml

7. Conclusions

without strategy, based more on emotion than on reason, where explanations - from the same experts - change from day to day.

Our view and our judgment on Russia suffer from a total lack of culture and knowledge, which opens the door to crude prejudices, as shown by the words of Alain Bauer on *France 5 about the* attitude of Russia towards the European Union:

> *Moscow's vision of Europe, since the fall of the Wall [of Berlin], which was not the end of the Soviet Union, but its retraction around its Russian core, is: [...] we have tried to work with you, you are soft, you have tried to plunder us, you do not exist, so for us you are not even representative of anything, you are a mop and nothing more [...], and basically we allow ourselves everything that is allowed until the moment when you express real power to us [...].*[355]

Thus, we have simply replaced in our minds the word "USSR" with "Russia". This is a simplistic view of history and a profound misunderstanding of Russia, the USSR, their respective leaders and their doctrines, as well as of the spirit of the Russian population, whose confidence in their government is much greater than that of the French.

The real challenge of the future will be the growing importance of Asia, at the expense of the West. Since the end of the Cold War, Russia has been asking for a rapprochement with Europe, which is why it has attached itself to the mechanisms that bind the Eurasian continent, such as the OSCE. However, under the influence of the United States, which wants neither a strong Europe nor a strong Russia, we have widened the gap. At present, we are only pushing Russia into the

---

355. Alain Bauer, in the program "C dans l'air" of February 10, 2021, ("Poutine met l'Europe à cran #cdanslair 10.02.2021", *France 5/YouTube*, February 11, 2021) (08'40").

arms of China, as Dostoyevsky predicted back in 1881: *"It is time to turn away from this ungrateful Europe. Our future is in Asia."*[356]

We conduct international relations based more on prejudice than on facts. To restore a more balanced perception of events, the deconstruction of fake news and "conspiracies" is necessary and *fact-checkers* could have a decisive role in this. The problem is that those who have taken on this role do so in a partisan manner and without a clear methodology. For example, *Conspiracy Watch* does not use a rigorous definition of conspiracism, mixing for example the notions of *"belief"* and *"conspiracy"*, which sometimes leads to denouncing conspiracies that are not conspiracies, taking into account only the information that supports its accusations and excluding the others[357]. Instead of objectively analyzing the facts, one substitutes a construction, which is nothing other than a form of conspiracy, even if it is the dominant opinion. For the plot *attributed to* the Russian government to eliminate Navalny is indeed... a plot! *Quis custodiet ipsos custodes?*

We will draw the final word from a June 2018 UK *Integrity Initiative* document on how to combat Russian disinformation, which should inspire the media outlets cited in this book and remind them of the Munich Charter of Ethics[358] :

> *Another obstacle to combating disinformation is the fact that some Kremlin-backed stories are factually true [...]. Responding to inconvenient truths, as opposed to pure propaganda, is naturally more problematic.* [359]

---

356. *The Complete Works of Fyodor Dostoyevsky: Novels, Short Stories and Autobiographical Writings (Unabridged)*, e-artnow, 24 May 2015.

357. Antoine Hasday, *op. cit.*

358. Or Declaration of the Duties and Rights of Journalists, 24 November 1971.

359. *Upskilling to Upscale: Unleashing the Capacity of Civil Society to Counter Disinformation*, Final Report, June 2018, p. 55 (paragraph 5.3).

8. Appendix

1. Report by doctors at the Charité Hospital in Berlin, published in the medical journal *The Lancet*, December 22, 2020

2. Appendix to the report by doctors at the Charité Hospital in Berlin, published in the medical journal *The Lancet*, December 22, 2020

3. Summary of the Report *on Activities Carried out in* Support of a *Request for Technical Assistance by Germany* (*Technical Assistance Visit* - TAV/01/20), Note By The Technical Secretariat, OPCW, 6 October 2020 (S/1906/2020)

4. Extract from the classified report of the Swedish laboratory

5. Message of support for the January 23, 2021 protesters from Ned Price, spokesperson for the U.S. State Department

Case Report

Novichok nerve agent poisoning

*David Steindl, Wolfgang Boehmerle, Roland Körner, Damaris Praeger, Marcel Haug, Jens Nee, Adrian Schreiber, Franziska Scheibe,
Katharina Demin, Philipp Jacoby, Rudolf Tauber, Sven Hartwig, Matthias Endres, Kai-Uwe Eckardt*

On Aug 20, 2020, a 44-year-old man who was previously healthy suddenly became confused and began to sweat heavily on a domestic flight in Russia approximately 10 min after departure; he vomited, collapsed, and lost consciousness. After an emergency landing, the man was admitted to the toxicology unit of a local hospital in Omsk, Russia, approximately 2 h after symptom onset. According to the discharge report, the patient presented comatose with hypersalivation and increased diaphoresis and was diagnosed to have respiratory failure, myoclonic status, disturbed carbohydrate metabolism, electrolyte disorders, and metabolic encephalopathy. Therapeutic measures included intubation, mechanical ventilation, and unspecified drugs for symptom control and neuroprotection. On Aug 22, 2020, the patient was transferred by a German air ambulance to the Charité-Universitätsmedizin Berlin at the request of his family. Severe poisoning with a cholinesterase inhibitor was subsequently diagnosed. 2 weeks later, the German Government announced that a laboratory of the German armed forces designated by the Organization for the Prohibition of Chemical Weapons (OPCW) had identified an organophosphorus nerve agent from the novichok group in blood samples collected immediately after the patient's admission to Charité,[1] a finding that was subsequently confirmed by the OPCW.[2] Here, we report clinical details of this case.

Clinical course

Approximately 31 h after symptom onset, a doctor from the German air ambulance crew had temporary access to the patient and recorded bradycardia (44 beats per min [bpm]), hypothermia (34·4°C), wide pupils non-reactive to light, and intermittent myoclonus under sedation with propofol, the only obvious drug given at that time. Peripheral oxygen saturation was 100% while the patient was on pressure-regulated volume-control ventilation with low positive end-expiratory pressure and a fractional concentration of oxygen in inspired air (FiO_2) of 30%. 16 h later, when the patient was handed over to the German air ambulance crew for transportation to Berlin, his condition had slightly improved (pupils constricted, heart rate 59 bpm). Propofol was again the only drug administered at that time.

During subsequent airborne transport in an EpiShuttle isolation system (EpiGuard, Oslo, Norway), the patient received propofol, fentanyl, and crystalloids and continued to be ventilated with 30% FiO_2. On arrival at an intensive care unit at Charité, approximately 55 h after symptom onset, the patient was deeply comatose, with mild bradycardia (51 bpm, subsequently declining to 33 bpm), hypersalivation, hypothermia (33·5°C), increased diaphoresis and small pupils not reactive to light, decreased

brainstem reflexes, hyperactive deep tendon reflexes, and pyramidal signs. Laboratory analyses showed substantially decreased levels in plasma of butyrylcholinesterase (also called pseudocholinesterase) and increased levels of amylase, lipase, high-sensitivity troponin T, and sodium in plasma (appendix p 1). Based on clinical and laboratory findings, severe cholinesterase inhibition was diagnosed and the patient was started on atropine and obidoxime (250 mg bolus followed by continuous administration of 750 mg per day). Cholinergic signs returned to normal within 1 h after the onset of this antidotal therapy. Analgo-sedation with sufentanil and propofol was supplemented with midazolam for neuroprotection.[3]

Toxicological analysis and drug screening in blood and urine samples obtained on admission to the intensive care unit at Charité identified several drugs, including atropine, which we attributed to the previous treatment the patient had received in the intensive care unit in Omsk before the medical transfer to Germany (appendix p 2). Testing for cholinesterase status[4] in a specialised external laboratory showed complete inhibition of acetylcholinesterase in red blood cells, thereby confirming the exposure to a cholinesterase inhibitor, and no evidence for reactivation by obidoxime or free unbound cholinesterase inhibitor in plasma (appendix p 3). Accordingly, obidoxime was stopped after 1 day.[5] Atropine was continued for 10 days and titrated to suppress cholinergic symptoms (figure 1). On day 5, the patient developed a fever that was treated with external cooling for 9 days and subsequently with antipyretic therapy using pethidine, metamizole, and paracetamol. Intermittent myoclonic muscular contractions, predominately of the thoracic and abdominal muscles, responded poorly to atropine and increased sedation and persisted for up to 15 days.

Cranial CT and MRI scans, analysis of cerebrospinal fluid, short-latency somatosensory evoked potentials, and plasma neuron-specific enolase concentration on day 4 were all within normal ranges, and an electro-encephalogram was consistent with sedation. Electrophysiological examinations showed the specific kind of dysfunction of neuromuscular transmission that is typical for cholinesterase inhibition. Repetitive responses were noted after a single supramaximal electrical stimulus (figure 2A). Repeated nerve stimulation showed a decrement-increment response pattern at frequencies of 10 Hz or greater, which was more pronounced at higher stimulation frequencies (figure 2B, 2C), consistent with blockade of neuromuscular transmission caused by depolarisation.[6] Stimulated single-fibre electromyography showed prolonged variation in the time between action potentials of the same motor unit, which is called jitter

Published Online
December 22, 2020
https://doi.org/10.1016/
S0140-6736(20)32644-1

See Online/Comment
https://doi.org/10.1016/
S0140-6736(20)32749-5

Department of Nephrology
and Medical Intensive Care
(D Steindl MD, R Körner MD,
J Nee MD, A Schreiber MD,
Prof K-U Eckardt MD),
Department of Neurology
(W Boehmerle MD,
F Scheibe MD,
K Demin Dr rer medic,
Prof M Endres MD), Department
of Cardiology and Angiology
(D Praeger MD, M Haug MD),
Institute of Legal Medicine and
Forensic Sciences
(S Hartwig MD), and Institute of
Laboratory Medicine, Clinical
Chemistry and
Pathobiochemistry
(Prof R Tauber MD),
Charité-Universitätsmedizin
Berlin, Berlin, Germany; Flight
Ambulance International,
Nürnberg, Germany
(P Jacoby MD); Labor Berlin
Charité Vivantes GmbH, Berlin,
Germany (Prof R Tauber)

Correspondence to:
Prof Kai-Uwe Eckardt,
Department of Nephrology and
Medical Intensive Care,
Charité-Universitätsmedizin
Berlin, 10117 Berlin, Germany
nephro-intensiv@charite.de

See Online for appendix

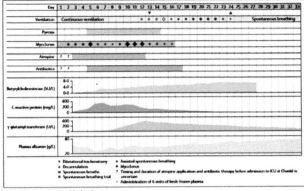

Day	1	2	3	4	5	6	7	8	9	10	11	12	13	14	15	16	17	18	19	20	21	22	23	24	25	26	27	28	29	30	31	32	33

Figure 1: Schematic presentation of the clinical course
Figure shows selected clinical findings, treatment aspects, and laboratory values during the patient's stay in intensive care (days 1–25) and on a regular hospital ward (days 26–33). Symbol sizes provide a semiquantitative estimate. Trends of laboratory findings recorded at Charité are displayed as area charts; values are provided in the appendix (p 4).

(figure 2D). These findings improved continuously within the next 7 days (figure 2A, 2C, 2D).

During the period in the intensive care unit at Charité, the patient temporarily showed signs of systemic inflammation and increases in liver enzymes (figure 1; appendix p 4). Activity of butyrylcholinesterase in plasma started to increase on day 4 but plateaued on day 6 at levels below normal, which prompted us to administer 6 units of fresh-frozen plasma; this transfusion led to a pronounced increase in activity with no subsequent decline, thus excluding consumption of butyrylcholinesterase by unbound inhibitory nerve agent in blood, consistent with findings of in vitro testing (appendix p 3). On day 10, the spontaneous increase in plasma butyrylcholinesterase activity resumed, and values within the normal range were reached on day 20 (appendix p 4). By comparison, activity of acetylcholinesterase in red blood cells recovered more slowly and only partly until day 21 (appendix p 3). The patient's haemoglobin concentration dropped from 12·2 g/dL to 7·5 g/dL and recovered after intravenous iron and oral folate supplementation.

In skin swabs obtained on admission to the intensive care unit at Charité, we noted colonisation with five different multidrug-resistant bacteria: Staphylococcus aureus, Acinetobacter baumannii complex, Pseudomonas aeruginosa, Escherichia coli, and Klebsiella pneumoniae. Microbial characterisation of subsequent rectal swabs

and urine samples showed two different variants of K pneumoniae. Based on these findings, we used antibiotics very reluctantly. A urinary tract infection with K pneumoniae was treated with co-trimoxazole, and a possible bloodstream infection with Staphylococcus epidermidis was treated with a 4-day course of vancomycin. CT on admission and plain chest radiography on days 3, 5, 9, 10, and 13 showed no clear signs of pulmonary infiltration. Because of purulent bronchoalveolar fluid in conjunction with increased levels of C-reactive protein, the patient received colistin inhalations for 9 days, subsequently tapered to prophylactic doses.

During the patient's stay in intensive care at Charité, gas exchange was never severely impaired. FiO₂ was usually below 40%, except on day 9, when it was temporarily increased to 50%. We did a percutaneous dilatational tracheostomy on day 13 in anticipation of complicated weaning. On day 12, the patient started to breathe spontaneously (figure 1) and could subsequently be weaned from mechanical ventilation completely by day 24. He gradually recovered from a delirium and was mobilised and transferred to a regular hospital ward on day 26. At discharge on day 33, a neurological examination showed enhanced physiological tremor and hyperactive deep tendon reflexes but neither pyramidal signs nor evidence of polyneuropathy. Neuropsychological testing performed in Russian, the patient's native language, showed subtle

www.thelancet.com Published online December 22, 2020 https://doi.org/10.1016/S0140-6736(20)32644-1

impairments in processing speed and verbal fluency, which had completely resolved 3 weeks later. At the last follow-up visit on day 55 we found near-complete recovery of neurological, neuropsychological, and neurophysiological findings without evidence of polyneuropathy.

Discussion

Novichoks are a group of nerve agents developed in the former Soviet Union in the 1980s.[?] Five recent cases of novichok poisoning, including one fatal, have been reported in the UK.[5,6] However, up to now, no clinical details have been published.

Identification of an individual organophosphorus compound is a complex and time-consuming process.[4] In fact, ascertaining the involvement of a novichok agent and its biotransformation products in this case was only achieved several days after establishing the diagnosis of cholinesterase inhibitor poisoning and did not affect therapeutic decisions.

Organophosphorus nerve agents exert the same mechanism of action as do organophosphorus pesticides (ie, inhibition of acetylcholinesterase) and clinical management is largely based on experience with organophosphorus pesticide poisonings, which still pose a major health burden in southeast Asia, with more than 100000 deaths per year.[8] Clinical diagnosis of organophosphorus poisoning should be straightforward. The range of findings caused by overstimulation of muscarinic and nicotinic receptors seen in our patient was in line with published literature: miosis, conjunctival injection, hypersalivation, diaphoresis, bradycardia, and elevation of plasma lipase and amylase, which are attributed to pancreatic and salivary gland stimulation, hyperactive deep tendon reflexes, pyramidal signs, and prolonged muscular hyperactivity.[9] Moreover, we observed typical pathological changes in electrophysiology and single-fibre electromyography studies.[10,11] After normalisation of neuromuscular transmission, the patient started to breathe spontaneously on day 12.

Tests for butyrylcholinesterase activity, which are primarily used as a liver function test, are widely available in clinical routine practice and are usually the only laboratory parameter to confirm a clinical diagnosis of organophosphorus poisoning. The cholinesterase status provides additional important information for therapeutic decisions, such as the presence of unbound acetylcholinesterase inhibitor in patient's plasma and the possibility to reactivate organophosphorus-acetylcholinesterase conjugates with a particular oxime (appendix p 3).[4] In fact, absence of inhibitory activity in our patient's plasma in conjunction with inability to reactivate acetylcholinesterase in red blood cells prompted early termination of obidoxime. Consistent with findings of experimental and clinical studies, sufficient muscle function enabling spontaneous breathing on day 21 correlated with approximately 30% activity of acetylcholinesterase in red blood cells (figure 1; appendix p 3).[11]

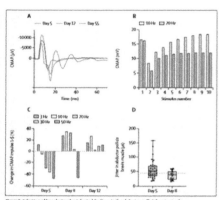

Figure 2: Selection of key electrophysiological findings in the abductor pollicis brevis muscle
(A) Repetitive responses were noted after a single supramaximal electrical stimulus, which disappeared at follow up. On day 55, normalised CMAP was seen. (B) Repetitive nerve stimulation of the median nerve on day 5 showed a decrement-increment pattern at frequencies >10 Hz, which was more pronounced at higher stimulation frequencies. (C) this finding continuously improved within the next 7 days. (D) Stimulated single-fibre electromyography with concentric needles showed increased jitter; line shows median, boxes the IQR, and error bars the range; dashed line represents upper limit of normal for individual jitter values. CMAP=compound motor action potential.

Additional findings with less clear pathophysiology have previously been described in organophosphorus poisoning. Among these was a refractory disturbance of thermoregulation with initial hypothermia followed by fever. Hypothermia during the early course might, in part, have been caused by increased diaphoresis, whereas side-effects of atropine, infectious complications, and unknown factors are considered to cause subsequent fever.[10] We also recorded a transient rise of troponin in conjunction with repolarisation disturbances on electrocardiogram in the presence of normal echocardiography, consistent with cardiotoxicity of nerve agents.[9] Signs of hepatic injury with increases of aminotransferases and γ glutamyl transferase have also previously been reported[6,2] and, in part, been attributed to obidoxime,[9] which our patient received for less than 24 h. An unexplained finding seen in this case was pronounced transient hypoalbuminaemia, which could not be attributed to enteric or renal loss or impaired liver function.

Our patient had a very favourable outcome. Presumably, intubation and mechanical ventilation within 2–3 h of symptom onset and absence of preceding severe hypoxia were decisive. Onset and duration of atropine therapy during the first 2 days remain unclear.

3

124

The Navalny case

Fortunately, despite a high risk for aspiration during the initial period of unconsciousness, and colonisation with several multidrug-resistant bacteria, the patient did not develop severe infection. His good health status before the poisoning probably favoured his recovery.

Contributors

DS and K-UF wrote the first draft of the report, coordinated internal revision, and prepared the submitted version. All authors contributed to data collection, data analysis, and data interpretation. RK, DP, MH, JN, AS and PJ were responsible for defined periods of treatment. WB, FS, and ME performed neurological and neurophysiological assessments. KD and ME did neuropsychological assessments. RT was responsible for clinical chemistry. SH did toxicological analyses. All authors vouch for accuracy of the data. DS and K-UF had unlimited access to all clinical data and reports.

Declaration of interests

We declare no competing interests.

Acknowledgments

This report was prepared using internal resources without specific funding. We gratefully acknowledge the support from many colleagues in the assessment and interdisciplinary management of this case, including members of the Bundeswehr Institute of Pharmacology and Toxicology in Munich, Germany, who did repetitive measurements of butyrylcholinesterase, acetylcholinesterase in red blood cells, and cholinesterase status and gave toxicological advice.

References

1 Seibert S. Statement by the Federal Government on the Navalny case. Sept 2, 2020. https://www.bundeskanzlerin.de/bkin-en/homepage/statement-by-the-federal-government-on-the-navalny-case-1783882 (accessed Dec 3, 2020).

2 OPCW Technical Secretariat. Summary of the report on activities carried out in support of a request for technical assistance by Germany (technical assistance visit—TAV/01/20). Oct 6, 2020. https://www.opcw.org/sites/default/files/documents/2020/10/s-1906-2020%28e%29.pdf (accessed Dec 3, 2020).

3 Hulse EJ, Haslam JD, Emmett SR, Woolley T. Organophosphorus nerve agent poisoning: managing the poisoned patient. Br J Anaesth 2019; 123: 457–63.

4 Thiermann H, Mast U, Klimmek R, et al. Cholinesterase status, pharmacokinetics and laboratory findings during obidoxime therapy in organophosphate poisoned patients. Hum Exp Toxicol 1997; 16: 473–80.

5 Amend N, Langgartner J, Siegert M, et al. A case report of cholinesterase inhibitor poisoning: cholinesterase activities and analytical methods for diagnosis and clinical decision making. Arch Toxicol 2020; 94: 2239–42.

6 Maselli RA, Leung C. Analysis of neuromuscular transmission failure induced by anticholinesterases. Ann N Y Acad Sci 1993; 681: 402–04.

7 Vale JA, Marrs TC, Maynard RL. Novichok: a murderous nerve agent attack in the UK. Clin Toxicol 2018; 56: 1093–97.

8 OPCW Technical Secretariat. Summary of the report on activities carried out in support of a request for technical assistance by the United Kingdom of Great Britain and Northern Ireland (technical assistance visit TAV/01/18 and TAV/03/18/18 "Amesbury Incident"). Sep 4, 2018. https://www.opcw.org/sites/default/files/documents/2018/09/s-1671-2018%28e%29.pdf (accessed Dec 3, 2020).

9 John H, van der Schans MJ, Koller M, et al. Fatal sarin poisoning in Syria 2013: forensic verification within an international laboratory network. Forensic Toxicol 2018; 36: 61–71.

10 Mew EJ, Padmanathan P, Konradsen F, et al. The global burden of fatal self-poisoning with pesticides 2006–15: systematic review. J Affect Disord 2017; 219: 93–104.

11 Grob D. The manifestations and treatment of poisoning due to nerve gas and other organic phosphate anticholinesterase compounds. AMA Arch Intern Med 1956; 98: 221–39.

12 Besser R, Gutmann L, Dillmann U, Weidemann LS, Hopf HC. End-plate dysfunction in acute organophosphate intoxication. Neurology 1989; 39: 561–67.

13 Thiermann H, Zilker T, Eyer F, Felgenhauer N, Eyer P, Worek F. Monitoring of neuromuscular transmission in organophosphate pesticide-poisoned patients. Toxicol Lett 2009; 191: 297–304.

14 Thiermann H, Eyer P, Worek F. Muscle force and acetylcholinesterase activity in mouse hemidiaphragms exposed to paraoxon and treated by oximes in vitro. Toxicology 2010; 272: 46–51.

15 Moffatt A, Mohammed F, Eddleston M, Azher S, Eyer P, Buckley NA. Hypothermia and fever after organophosphorus poisoning in humans: a prospective case series. J Med Toxicol 2010; 6: 179–85.

16 Chu YS, Kim H, Go J, et al. Features of myocardial injury in severe organophosphate poisoning. Clin Toxicol 2014; 52: 873–79.

17 Yu S, Yu S, Zhang L, et al. Efficacy and outcomes of lipid resuscitation on organophosphate poisoning patients: a systematic review and meta-analysis. Am J Emerg Med 2019; 37: 1611–17.

18 Eyer F, Worek F, Eyer P, et al. Obidoxime in acute organophosphate poisoning: 1—clinical effectiveness. Clin Toxicol 2009; 47: 798–806.

8. Appendix

Appendix 2 - Appendix to the report of the Charité doctors (Berlin)

THE LANCET

Supplementary appendix

This appendix formed part of the original submission and has been peer reviewed. We post it as supplied by the authors.

Supplement to: Steindl D, Boehmerle W, Körner R, et al. Novichok nerve agent poisoning. Lancet 2020; published online Dec 22. http://dx.doi.org/10.1016/S0140-6736(20)32644-1.

Parameter	Value	Reference range	Unit
Glucose	95	74-106	mg/dL
C-peptide	2.05	1.10-4.40	µg/L
Insulin	3.66	2.60-24.80	mU/L
TSH	1.60	0.27-4.20	mU/L
Plasma sodium	**154**	136-145	mmol/L
Plasma potassium	4.2	3.5-4.5	mmol/L
Plasma chloride	**120**	98-107	mmol/L
Plasma calcium	2.21	2.15-2.50	mmol/L
Creatinine	0.91	0.70-1.20	mg/dL
Cystatin c	0.98	0.47-1.09	mg/L
eGFR cystatin	87.6		mL/min
Urea	40	17-48	mg/dL
Creatine kinase	169	<190	U/L
Creatine kinase-MB	**49.7**	<24.0	U/L
High-sensitivity troponin T	**16**	<14	ng/L
Myoglobin	**462**	28-72	µg/L
Bilirubin	0.26	<1.20	mg/dL
Alanine aminotransferase	18	<41	U/L
Alkaline phosphatase	70	40-130	U/L
Gamma glutamyl transferase	16	8-61	U/L
Albumin	**31.9**	35.0-52.0	g/L
Butyryl cholinesterase	**0.42**	5.32-12.92	kU/L
Lactate dehydrogenase	**261**	135-250	U/L
Amylase	**385**	28-100	U/L
Lipase	**111**	13-60	U/L
C-reactive protein	**47.8**	<5.0	mg/L
Procalcitonin	0.32	<0.5	µg/L
Total leukocytes	**16.56**	3.9-10.5	/nL
Neutrophils	**14.29**	1.50-7.70	/nL
Erythrocytes	**4.0**	4.3-5.8	/pL
Haemoglobin	**12.2**	13.5-17.0	g/dL
Haematocrit	**0.351**	0.395-0.505	1/1
Platelets	273	150-370	/nL
INR	1.24	0.9-1.25	
aPTT	36.3	26.0-40.0	s
Urinary protein/creatinine ratio	**295**	<140	mg/g
Urinary albumin/creatinine ratio	**25**	<20	mg/g

Appendix S1: Laboratory values on admission.

8. Appendix

Substance	Urine	Blood
Fentanyl	positive	positive
Sufentanil	positive	positive
Morphine	positive	negative
Ofloxacin	positive	negative
Levofloxacin	positive	positive
Atropine	positive	negative
Gabapentin	positive	negative
Urapidil	positive	negative
Amantadine	positive	negative
Pilocarpine	positive	negative
Lithium	not performed	positive
Rocuronium	positive	negative
Alcohol	not performed	negative
Diazepam	negative	positive
Nordazepam	positive	positive
Oxazepam	positive	negative
Temazepam	positive	positive
Gamma-hydroxybutyrate	negative	not performed
Pentobarbital	negative	positive
Thiopental	negative	positive

Appendix S2: Results of local toxicology and medication tests in blood and urine samples obtained on arrival of the patient at Charité – Universitätsmedizin Berlin (day 3). A hair sample obtained on day 4 confirmed the presence of several of the compounds detected in blood and urine and, in addition, revealed the presence of Tropicamide. Results of toxicology analyses conducted in a special laboratory of the armed forces are not included.

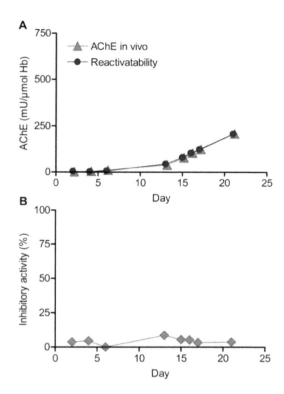

Appendix S3. Repetitive determination of the cholinesterase status in patient blood.[4] The timeline is given in days after the supposed poisoning of the patient. (A) RBC-AChE activity in whole blood dilutions (AChE in vivo) and after incubation of whole blood dilutions with 100 µM obidoxime ex vivo (reactivatability). (B) The presence of a cholinesterase inhibitor was determined by incubation of patient plasma with test AChE (inhibitory activity).

8. Appendix

Appendix S4: Laboratory findings during the ICU stay at Charité (days 3-25), the subsequent stay on a regular hospital ward (days 26-33) and a subsequent visit as an outpatient.

Parameter	Unit	Reference range	3	4	5	6	7	8	9	10	11	12	13	14	15	16	17	18	19	20	21	22	23	24	25	26	28	29	30	33	42
Creatine kinase	U/L	<190	169	939	442	131	48	44	36	47	89	73	126	75	135	129	88	67	40	31	16	:	:	:	:	:	:	:	:	33	42
High-sensitivity troponin T	ng/L	<14	16	28	21	15	10	9	:	9	12	9	:	12	15	11	12	15	18	16	16	:	:	:	:	:	:	:	25	22	33
Alanine aminotransferase	U/L	<41	16	22	18	15	16	22	35	40	49	48	52	44	37	46	53	80	90	97	83	:	56	50	38	36	29	25	21	:	19
Alkaline phosphatase	U/L	40-130	70	59	56	60	65	180	197	238	270	180	166	160	143	133	111	111	107	111	107	:	80	80	87	93	93	87	:	:	76
Gamma glutamyl transferase	U/L	8-61	16	18	17	28	43	135	239	321	410	349	347	297	285	276	254	255	226	221	189	:	162	168	143	147	121	120	93	59
Albumin	g/L	35.0-52.0	31.9	29.0	29.2	23.3	25.2	29.1	25.4	29.3	30.8	29.2	29.4	29.6	29.1	:	:	32.8	34.9	32.1	:	:	34.7	37.2	34.5	37.1	37.6	:	30.4	47.3
Butyryl cholinesterase	kU/L	6.32-12.92	0.41	0.71	1.34	1.20	2.97	2.93	2.74	3.21	3.59	3.75	4.09	4.32	4.57	4.88	4.76	5.22	5.28	5.45	5.40	5.23	5.94	6.32	6.03	6.80	6.80	7.06	:	0.80
Lipase	U/L	13-60	111	44	19	11	16	31	:	43	44	41	33	37	40	127	148	176	121	172	:	189	113	:	:	:	:	:	:
C-reactive protein	mg/L	<5.0	48	95	138	324	353	255	252	263	278	182	134	129	116	89	85	69	57	49	33	20	15	12	7	5	4	1	1	<0.6
Procalcitonin	µg/L	<0.5	0.32	0.28	0.20	2.77	3.95	2.53	1.64	1.14	0.76	0.59	0.51	0.37	0.28	0.17	0.17	0.15	0.16	0.14	0.10	0.07	0.05	0.04	0.04	0.03	:	:	0.71
Total leukocytes	/nL	3.9-10.5	16.6	6.96	5.15	9.43	10.3	9.03	11.1	10.9	11.1	9.54	9.57	11.9	12.7	13.4	9.2	10.1	10.9	8.68	8.43	7.38	7.34	8.02	6.84	6.99	6.97	:	7.46	5.6
Haemoglobin	g/dL	13.5-17.0	12.2	11.9	11.2	10.0	9.9	8.0	8.0	8.2	8.4	8.1	7.9	8.1	7.7	7.7	7.5	8.6	8.8	8.7	8.8	8.5	9.3	9.3	9.2	10.8	11.2	11.4	12.9
Platelets	/nL	150-370	273	273	180	181	195	177	208	264	304	395	450	536	576	621	661	755	821	763	782	714	774	733	651	746	659	533	435	322
Urinary protein/creatinine ratio	mg/g	<140	295	:	:	:	:	337	422	:	:	:	:	288	:	:	:	:	:	:	:	:	:	:	:	72
Urinary albumin/creatinine ratio	mg/g	<20	25	:	:	:	:	21	16	:	:	:	:	15	:	:	:	:	:	:	:	:	:	:	:	0

Annex 3 - OPCW Analysis Report

 **OPCW**   Technical Secretariat

S/1906/2020
6 October 2020
Original: ENGLISH

NOTE BY THE TECHNICAL SECRETARIAT

SUMMARY OF THE REPORT ON ACTIVITIES CARRIED OUT IN SUPPORT OF A REQUEST FOR TECHNICAL ASSISTANCE BY GERMANY (TECHNICAL ASSISTANCE VISIT – TAV/01/20)

1. The Government of Germany, in a communication to the OPCW Director-General on 4 September 2020, requested technical assistance from the OPCW Technical Secretariat (hereinafter "the Secretariat") under subparagraph 38(e) of Article VIII of the Chemical Weapons Convention (hereinafter the "Convention") in relation to the suspected poisoning of a Russian citizen, Mr Alexei Navalny, on 20 August 2020 in the Russian Federation. The German authorities informed the OPCW that Mr Navalny was being treated in a hospital in Berlin, Germany. The Director-General decided to dispatch a team to Germany for a technical assistance visit (TAV).

2. The TAV team deployed to Germany on 5 September 2020 and was briefed by the German authorities on the same day. The team was informed that the mission was restricted to the collection of biomedical samples from Mr Navalny. No other information was shared by the German authorities.

3. On 6 September 2020, the TAV team visited the Charité Hospital in Berlin. In the hospital's intensive care unit, the TAV team members confirmed Mr Navalny's identity against a photo-identification document presented to the team by the German authorities. In line with OPCW procedures, blood and urine sampling was conducted by the hospital staff under the direct supervision and continuous visual observation of the team members. The samples were maintained under OPCW chain of custody and transported to the OPCW Laboratory.

4. Upon receipt of a request from Germany on 11 September 2020, the OPCW Laboratory sent the samples to two laboratories designated by the Director-General for the analysis of biomedical samples.

5. The results of the analysis of biomedical samples conducted by the OPCW designated laboratories demonstrate that Mr Navalny was exposed to a toxic chemical acting as a cholinesterase inhibitor. The biomarkers of the cholinesterase inhibitor found in Mr Navalny's blood and urine samples have similar structural characteristics to the toxic chemicals belonging to schedules 1.A.14 and 1.A.15, which were added to the Annex on Chemicals to the Convention at the Twenty-Fourth Session of the Conference of the States Parties in November 2019. This cholinesterase inhibitor is not listed in the Annex on Chemicals to the Convention.

6. The biomarkers identified are contained in the classified report of the Secretariat.

- - - o - - -

CS-2020-2628(E) distributed 06/10/2020

8. Appendix

Appendix 4 - Report of the Swedish analyses

Collection of samples

Two blood samples were collected from the patient on the 5th of September 2020, ███████████. The two blood samples were collected into one Vacuette® tube for plasma separation (2.5 ml LH Lithium Heparin Separator, item No. 456010) and one Vacuette tube for serum separation (CAT Serum Separator Clot Activator, item No. 456010). Both samples were sealed and stored cold until sample preparation. ██████████████████████████

Directly after centrifugation about 2 ml of plasma from the Heparine separator tube was transferred to a new 15 ml centrifuge tube (Fisher Scientific). From the Serum Separator tube about 3 ml serum was transferred to a new 15 ml centrifuge tube.

Preparation and analysis of serum and plasma samples

██
████████████████████ The extracted butyrylcholinesterase (in 200 µl 5% formic acid solution) was digested with pepsin (50 µl of a 2 mg/ml solution in 5% formic acid) at +37°C for 2 hours. The remaining peptides were centrifuged through 3kDa MW cutoff filters (20 minutes at 14 000 G).

The filtrate, about 200 µl, was transferred to new analysis vials. From the plasma sample filtrate about 80 µl was dried under a gentle flow of nitrogen and then dissolved in 20 µl 5% formic acid before analysis. The serum filtrate was analysed directly without further sample preparation.

██

All samples were analysed by LC-MS/MS (MRM) on a Waters XevoXS coupled to an Acquity UHPLC.

██

Chromatographic settings: Column used was a Waters Acquity BEH C18, 2.1x50 mm, 1.7 µm, column temperature +30°C. Gradient elution with composition of A: 0.1% formic acid in water and B: 0.1 % formic acid in acetonitrile. Gradient Flow rate 0.2 ml/min. 0-1 min 2% B, 1-10 min linear gradient 2-50 % B, 10-10.1 min linear gradient 50-95 % B, 10.1-12 min 95 % B, 12-12.1 min 95-2 % B, 12.1-15 min 2 % B. Sample volume injected was 5 µl.

Results:

The presence ██████████████████████ was confirmed in the patient's blood ████████████████

Source : https://twitter.com/mazzenilsson/
status/1314600936497704960/photo/1

Appendix 5 -
U.S. State Department Message of Support
for January 23, 2021 Protesters

U.S. DEPARTMENT OF STATE

Office of the Spokesperson

For Immediate Release

STATEMENT BY NED PRICE, SPOKESPERSON

January 23, 2021

Protests in Russia

The United States strongly condemns the use of harsh tactics against protesters and journalists this weekend in cities throughout Russia. Prior to today's events, the Russian government sought to suppress the rights to peaceful assembly and freedom of expression by harassing protest organizers, threatening social media platforms, and pre-emptively arresting potential participants. This follows years of tightening restrictions on and repressive actions against civil society, independent media, and the political opposition.

Continued efforts to suppress Russians' rights to peaceful assembly and freedom of expression, the arrest of opposition figure Aleksey Navalny, and the crackdown on protests that followed are troubling indications of further restrictions on civil society and fundamental freedoms. Russians' rights to peaceful assembly and to participate in free and fair elections are enshrined not only in the country's constitution, but also in Russia's OSCE commitments, the Universal Declaration of Human Rights, and in its international obligations under the International Covenant on Civil and Political Rights.

We call on Russian authorities to release all those detained for exercising their universal rights and for the immediate and unconditional release of Aleksey Navalny. We urge Russia to fully cooperate with the international community's investigation into the poisoning of Aleksey Navalny and credibly explain the use of a chemical weapon on its soil.

The United States will stand shoulder-to-shoulder with our allies and partners in defense of human rights whether in Russia or wherever they come under threat.

# # #

Stay connected with the Office of Press Relations

Table of contents

Best sellers Max Milo Editions

Hitler's banker, Jean-François Bouchard

Confessions of a forger, Éric Piedoie Le Tiec

The Koran and the flesh, Ludovic-Mohamed Zahed

Governing by fake news, Jacques Baud

Governing by chaos, Collectif

A political history of food, Paul Ariès

Mad in U.S.A.: The ravages of the "American model", Michel Desmurget

Mondial soccer club geopolitics, Kévin Veyssière

Putin: Game master?, Jacques Braud

Treatise on the three impostors: Moses, Jesus, Muhammad, The Spirit of Spinoza

TV Lobotomy, Michel Desmurget